Leading with Gravitas

Unlock the
six keys to impact
and influence

Antoinette
Dale Henderson

Praise for *Leading with Gravitas*

Gravitas is the all-important but often elusive factor that we all seek to have. In writing this book, Antoinette Dale Henderson has, for the first time, given us an incredibly practical way to access it. Gravitas is an essential quality for success in business and in *Leading With Gravitas* it is possible to fully examine in detail and properly understand the different dimensions within it. Unlike other books on the subject, the analytical approach outlined, which is based on real life experiences from a broad range of leaders, allows the reader to gain a clear understanding of the vital components and not only how they currently perform against them but also what they can actually do to improve. This book is a must read for emerging leaders who are looking to increase their personal impact. For experienced leaders, its fresh perspective provides the opportunity to revisit and even challenge what may be otherwise taken for granted in this crucial but often evasive business skill.

Sarah Matthew, Joint CEO, Virgo Health & Joint MD,
Global Healthcare Practice, Golin

I admire the work and the study that Antoinette Dale Henderson has put into getting this important topic out into the world in the form that she has. There is no doubt that gravitas is needed in abundance right now and the good news is that it can be learnt. And Antoinette offers us simple and practical ways of learning it. Her background research is admirable and the logical way in which she presents this makes it easily accessible and available to anyone. I encourage you to read this and to take the learning she offers on board.

Sue Knight, author of *NLP At Work*

In today's fast paced life we often overlook the basics of what being a good leader is. This book provides a holistic and digestible approach on how to be an effective leader. A structured and valuable framework for young and seasoned leaders to gain insight into and continuously improve their verbal and non-verbal communication styles. A must read with good reference material you will come back to over and over again.

Mobina Salahuddin, Senior Manager, Deloitte UK

Leading with Gravitas is a wonderful resource for getting on in life. Few of us are born with the qualities needed to inspire others but as Antoinette Dale Henderson shows in her book many of these qualities can be acquired. *Leading With Gravitas* provides a well researched framework for self-assessment and action informed by the latest developments in psychology, contemporary case studies and lessons from the ancients. If you are on a quest to fulfil your potential by harnessing what you have to offer more effectively this book will give you the practical tools to realise your goals.

Margot James, Member of Parliament for Stourbridge, UK

Antoinette Dale Henderson demonstrates that she really understands the essence of gravitas and what it can mean for you and particularly for your business or career. Many writers have shared stories about leaders with gravitas, but she goes way beyond that. Her book gives you a simple yet comprehensive and flexible framework to develop your own gravitas to give you greater impact and influence.

Dave Clarke, CEO, NRG Business Networks

A very pragmatic and insightful read. This will be very helpful to a broad senior management segment who are looking to move into senior leadership roles.

Shrey Viranna, CEO, Discovery Health

Gravitas is a trait that is hard to define — someone's got it or they haven't. But that doesn't help a person to self-develop professionally and personally. This book provides a vocabulary, a methodology, tools and exercises to help recognise and cultivate these aspects in yourself, without helping you to 'fake it'. The real person stories lend great insights into how people from a range of sectors have overcome challenges. It could be especially helpful for Millennial emerging leaders and rising stars who may need to build their confidence to try new things. I especially liked the chapter on Authenticity. We're not automatonic conformists at the workplace. Encouraging leaders to embrace their passion and individuality is so important.

Brian Tjugum, Global Director, Health Impact at Weber Shandwick

Gravitas. Everybody wants it, few know how to get it. This is the very first time that I have seen that all-important quality broken down into meaningful components, combined with practical exercises to strengthen it in us all. A must read for anyone serious about making an impact!

Kelly Teasdale, Director, Global Brand Communications

Leading With Gravitas is an insightful read. It pushes all the right buttons on topics that will be equally useful in day to day life as within the working environment. Working in a position of leadership can often be a daunting and isolating experience. This book helps the reader grasp the tools necessary to unravel the code of great leadership.

Luke Dale Roberts, Chef and Entrepreneur

R3THINK PRESS

First published in Great Britain 2015
by Rethink Press (www.rethinkpress.com)

© Copyright Antoinette Dale Henderson

Images by Christopher Page
Photographs: Maria Green, Fotos by Faith

*To Zoë and Mia, with all my love,
admiration and gratitude.*

Contents

Preface

'I want to be all that I am
capable of becoming.'

• Katherine Mansfield •

In over 25 years of working in communications I've observed that it's leaders who articulate their message with clarity and confidence that make the most impact over the longest term. In times of change, what people are looking for is a leader with vision and integrity, someone who commands respect while being themselves, a voice that's heard without shouting: in short, a leader with gravitas.

Gravitas is important for anyone who wants to present a professional image at whatever stage in their career. It's crucial for planned occasions – delivering presentations, negotiating deals, getting promoted – but is just as essential day to day – leading teams, meeting new clients, or networking. Developing gravitas is particularly important for leaders, as it enables them to inspire others through their personal qualities and stand out from the crowd without being fake or compromising their values or beliefs.

It is rare for people to be born with this ability. If you think of the world's most memorable leaders, few were natural communicators. Most of them earned their right to speech through a process of self-discovery and time spent honing their delivery. Winston Churchill described himself at the early part of his career as having a speech impediment which he worked hard to overcome. Margaret Thatcher hired a voice coach who taught her how to speak more slowly, and took advice from Laurence Olivier, who encouraged her to project more personality into her speeches.[1]

Most of us have, at some point, experienced the challenge of not being able to express ourselves effectively. The heart-sinking moment of knowing that we didn't quite do ourselves justice. Or that annoying feeling when the point you've just made is brushed aside, only to be fervently agreed with when made by someone else.

It may be that you have experienced some of the challenges faced by the managers and leaders who have come to me for coaching in recent years.

John: As CEO of a software company one of my main roles is delivering motivational presentations to the team. Although I am proud of my achievements I have always had a nagging voice in my head telling me that I haven't truly earned the right to my position. When I stand up and present, in the back of my mind I have an irrational fear that someone will find me out and make a fool of me in front of the whole company. I suspect that, because of my weak delivery, my team don't see me as the strong leader I know I can be.

Melissa: I am a Director in a global communications agency. I have been told that to be promoted to the next level I need to increase my gravitas and personal profile. I have no idea what gravitas is, whether it can be learnt, and if so, what I need to do to develop it. I know that to get promoted I will need to stand out from my peers.

[1] http://www.telegraph.co.uk/news/politics/margaret-thatcher/8999746/How-Maggie-Thatcher-was-remade.html

Melissa: However, I feel uncomfortable taking on what feels like a superior role to my colleagues, and don't want to come across as pushy, fake or arrogant.

Simon: I was recently interviewed for a position in a company I have admired for years. Although on paper I was more than qualified for the job I walked out knowing they would not invite me back. I was very nervous at the beginning of the interview. They asked me a question and my mind went blank. I then rambled on for what felt like hours. If only I could have relaxed, got my message straight, they would have seen the real me, and I'm sure I would have gone through to the next stage.

What united these people was a desire to fulfil their potential, a drive to step fully into their role of leader. What they all had in common was a need for inner confidence and the ability to communicate their message with impact.

Gravitas is a topic that's been close to my heart for many years. During my career in communications we'd refer to it as though it were a passport to senior positions. Through my work in leadership development and executive coaching, it's become more and more pertinent as people feel the pressure to step up, be taken seriously, and respond to demands to deliver faster results earlier in their career.

Gravitas is traditionally associated with statesmanlike qualities. Classic examples are silver-haired men with the wisdom of age and the senior positions to go with it. Like a fine wine, their gravitas has matured over time. However, in today's competitive and fast-paced environment people are expected to display it at a younger age. There's no time to simply allow it to develop.

I have written this book to demystify gravitas, maximise its potential as a leadership skill and accelerate its development. My goal is to provide you with the tools to uncover your own gravitas, find your unique voice, and develop the strength to lead in whatever situation you find yourself.

As part of my research I've interviewed and modelled leaders from diverse backgrounds and cultures to define what gravitas represents today. From this, I've created a model that makes the intangible nature of gravitas tangible, uniting six qualities which together convey a strong and powerful version of you.

Throughout this book we will explore what gravitas means for today's leaders and how they use their individuality to make a lasting impression. We'll consider people who break the traditional silver-haired model of gravitas, people who inspire confidence and command respect by revealing their authentic personalities. Most importantly, we'll look at what you can do to define your own gravitas and leadership style.

At this point, I'd like to highlight that to get the most out of this book, you will need to put the work in. I encourage you to not only read the chapters, but also apply the tools and techniques and seek feedback on your progress. Although it will not be possible, or advisable, for you to take everything on board at once, I have found through the *Leading with Gravitas* programme that it is the people who immerse themselves and go beyond their comfort zone who go the furthest, fastest. I encourage you to do the same.

I wish you all the best in reading this book and applying the learning to your career and personal development. I look forward to hearing how building gravitas has helped you be the leader you were born to be, and achieve your purpose in your organisation and in life.

Antoinette Dale Henderson

Further information on the Leading with Gravitas programme, the Gravitas Profiling Questionnaire© and other useful resources can be found on the Leading with Gravitas website www.leadingwithgravitas.com

Understanding Gravitas

The word 'gravitas' has its roots in ancient Rome and was one of the virtues that Romans were expected to possess to fulfil their role in society, along with pietas, dignitas and virtus[2]. Gravitas is translated as weight, seriousness, solemnity, dignity and importance. It denotes a certain substance or depth of personality that elicits a feeling of respect and trust in others. The word is also linked to 'gravity', a centrifugal force that keeps you grounded and 'gravitate', an energy that attracts people to you.

In today's work environment it's not enough to rely on authority or title to lead others. What is required is an ability to communicate, collaborate, influence and develop meaningful relationships. Building gravitas enables leaders like you to command respect and increase their personal visibility. People with gravitas lead better, present better, communicate better and network better. In a competitive environment, leaders who know how to access this quality build stronger relationships, win more business, get promoted more quickly and get better results.

In researching this book, I examined the characteristics that leaders with gravitas share in the 21st century, characteristics that you can emulate if you are looking to develop your leadership style.

One of the first things I realised is that gravitas is defined not by how you see yourself, but by the perception of the people around you – your audiences – and so it is within their gift to bestow. However, although gravitas, like beauty, is in the eye of the beholder, the good news is that the extent to which people see gravitas in you *is* within your power to determine. If you feel worthy of people's attention and respect, you will be more likely to receive it.

---

[2] Pietas: translated as duty, loyalty and devotion; Dignitas: dignity, prestige and charisma; Virtus: valour, courage and worth.

As part of my research I found that there is no 'one size fits all' model of gravitas; that it encapsulates a multifaceted array of qualities and that people tend to value the qualities that they see, or would like to see, in themselves.

In examining people with gravitas I also found that some develop it over time and others have it naturally. Compare, for example, two employees at a City law firm, one of whom has gravitas with polish – impressive credentials and a powerful ability to command attention – and the other, who has none of the trappings, but an inherent ability to state the facts persuasively and with impact. Both have gravitas, both express it in very different ways.

At a fundamental level a leader with gravitas has spent time exploring who they are, and their unique purpose and direction in their organisation and life. Whether corporate or community leader, entrepreneur or business owner, they look beyond their immediate horizon to the world on a wider scale, and are willing to make a contribution that is beyond personal gain, working towards what they believe in without getting carried away by their own personal agenda. At the heart of gravitas is a sense of purpose.

In addition to possessing strong foundations, a leader with gravitas has the ability to communicate with conviction, earning admiration through their actions, words and ability to listen. This conviction gives them a certainty which inspires others: they know what they are there to achieve, their line of sight is focused on a compelling future and, as such, they 'walk their talk'. For them, gravitas reflects who they are on the inside, rather than how they think they should be to fit in. They share the belief of the late Steve Jobs who urged: 'Your time is limited, so don't waste it living someone else's life.'

In addition to a clear purpose and conviction I found that leaders with gravitas share a number of *internal* qualities that reflect their beliefs, values and personal identity, and *external* qualities that determine how they present themselves to the outside world and are experienced by others.

The internal qualities of gravitas include:

1 Self-awareness: an acknowledgment of your values, beliefs, identity and purpose; recognition of your strengths and limitations; an ongoing drive for self-development.

2 Expertise: an appreciation of, and belief in, your unique knowledge, experience and capabilities; a desire to become an expert in a chosen field; an ability to share your expertise eloquently.

3 Authenticity: an ability to remain true to your values and beliefs irrespective of external factors; a commitment to acting consistently and characteristically in all situations.

The external qualities of gravitas include:

4 Presence: an energy that emanates from a person; the ability to attract attention and make an impact through physical appearance, body language and voice.

5 Connection: an affinity with people; the art of building networks and relationships, creating rapport and communicating eloquently with a broad range of audiences.

6 Projection: an ability to 'switch on' your best self, expressing yourself confidently to the largest audiences.

These internal and external qualities are encapsulated in the Gravitas Wheel© and form the basis for this book.

The Gravitas Wheel©

This book has been designed to help you to build gravitas as a leader by focusing on the six internal and external qualities of the Gravitas Wheel©. Within each chapter you will find a range of models and tools which, when applied, will enhance your *Self-awareness*, *Expertise*, *Authenticity*, *Presence*, *Connection* and *Projection*. In applying these learnings you will expand your leadership style and the skills to communicate your message with gravitas.

The first step to developing your gravitas as a leader is to examine which qualities are strongest for you, and which might be holding you back. The Gravitas Wheel© is a unique tool that's been designed to help you explore your personal strengths, with the right hand side of the circle representing the inner qualities of gravitas, the left hand side representing the outer qualities, and the word 'Purpose' at the centre.

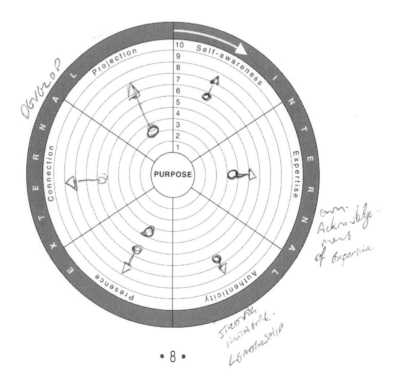

Starting with *Self-awareness* and working clockwise round the Wheel, begin by marking on each segment where you currently see yourself against each of the qualities, taking the centre of the Wheel as 0 and the outer edge as 10 and using the descriptions of each quality in this chapter as your guide. For example, if you feel like you have substantial expertise, but find it difficult to connect with your team, you might score yourself 8 in the *Expertise* segment and 4 in the *Connection* segment. If you have spent considerable time on self-reflection but find presenting to a large group challenging, you might score yourself 9 for *Self-awareness* and 3 for *Projection*. You can then mark on the Wheel where you would like to see yourself. So if you would like to enhance your ability to *Project*, score yourself 9 or 10 in that segment.[3]

The goal is not to score 10 for each – in fact, someone who scores themselves 10 in each component would probably appear too polished and slick to have real influence. The real goal is to identify which segments are inherently strong in you and which segments, if further developed, would enhance your leadership style and enable you to communicate with greater gravitas.

Once you have completed the Wheel, consider the following questions:
- In which segments do you score yourself highest and lowest?
- Are you stronger on the internal or external components of gravitas?
- Which segment/s are you not making the most of?
- Which segment/s would you like to develop further?

---

[3] For an online version of the Gravitas Wheel©, go to www.leadingwithgravitas.com/resources.

Using this book

Now that you have identified your current gravitas 'profile', you can focus on those areas you would like to develop. In the following chapters, we explore the six components of gravitas in turn, starting with the internal components – the foundations of your gravitas – and ending with the external components – how you express your gravitas to others. Although all the components are interconnected, it is not necessary to read each chapter in turn. If you prefer, you could begin with the areas which are a priority for you and go back to the other chapters afterwards.

Once you have read this book and completed the exercises, you will have a solid understanding of your unique leadership style and have at your fingertips a wealth of tips and techniques that you can use to communicate with impact.

In developing your gravitas and reflecting on your leadership you will begin to define your unique purpose, represented at the centre of the Wheel. This knowledge and skill will enable you to command respect, build loyalty and inspire trust, so that you can make a fundamental difference in your business and the world.

A snapshot of what you will get in each chapter

- Chapter 1 – Self-awareness: how to be confident with who you are. Here, we focus on the most important segment of the Gravitas Wheel©, the catalyst for personal growth and the launch pad for all the other segments. Using a selection of tools you will examine your unique strengths and purpose as a leader and in life.
- Chapter 2 – Expertise: how to maximise your unique abilities and receive the recognition you deserve. Expertise is a core component of gravitas. In this chapter, we look at what you can do to enhance your expertise and build a compelling profile that you can use in response to the 'so what do you do?' question.

- Chapter 3 – Authenticity: how to reveal your 'best self'. Authenticity comes as a result of self-awareness and a willingness to present yourself to the world as you are. In this chapter, we look at the concept of 'managed authenticity' and what you can do to keep progressing as an authentic leader.

- Chapter 4 – Presence: how to use your unique energy to stand out and be noticed. People with presence command attention just by being in a room. They hold an audience spell-bound and radiate an energy that inspires and attracts. In this chapter, we look at how you can develop presence and control the impact you're making to suit various situations.

- Chapter 5 – Connection: how to build strong and meaningful relationships. The way a person connects is the most tangible evidence of their gravitas. It encompasses and expresses the five previous components of the Wheel, creating an environment for your gravitas to be witnessed by others. Here, we look at developing a valuable and supportive network and how to build rapport and influence with integrity.

- Chapter 6 – Projection: how to amplify your message. Projection is the final segment of the Gravitas Wheel©, and the one that proclaims your gravitas most widely. In this chapter we explore how you can 'switch your gravitas on' when required and how you can use your body language and voice to project confidently, even to the largest audiences.

- Chapter 7 – Modelling Leaders with Gravitas: how to replicate excellence. Modelling is an invaluable technique for understanding and reproducing performance. In this chapter, we look at how you can model people with gravitas, so that you can turn what could be perceived as 'lucky' or 'gifted' behaviour into skills that you can reproduce at will.

Chapter 1

Self-awareness

'Look well into thyself; there is a source
of strength which will always spring
up if thou wilt always look there'

• Marcus Aurelius •

Self-awareness is the first internal quality associated with gravitas and the most important segment of the Gravitas Wheel©. When it comes to leadership, self-awareness is crucial. Without it you are blind to your potential, blind to your flaws, blind to how you come across and blind to your impact on others.

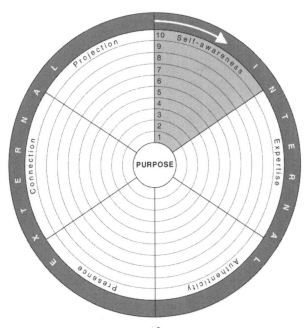

Self-awareness is the starting point for people who want to build their gravitas and acts like a touchstone throughout their progress. People with self-awareness understand the qualities that they – and only they – possess to fulfil a role. Through inner reflection and receptivity to feedback they appreciate and nurture their strengths and know how and when to use them. They are also honest about their weaknesses, aware of the internal thoughts and external forces that can block their progress and take responsibility for addressing them.

Having an in-depth understanding of who you are will have a massive impact on your ability to develop gravitas, giving you the evidence with which to share your *Expertise*, the clarity to be *Authentic*, the grounded-ness to convey *Presence*, the empathy to *Connect* and the confidence to *Project*.

In classic tales of knights' quests and heroes' journeys there comes a point where the lead character looks into himself and becomes aware of his personal mission and destiny in life. For modern day leaders like you, increased self-awareness can bring a greater sense of identity and purpose – beyond roles and responsibilities – and a recognition of the difference that you personally want to make in your lifetime.

As well as being important from a personal perspective, self-awareness can make a big difference to how you see yourself professionally. Becoming aware of the values and beliefs that are important to you and how they align with your company's vision, mission and values, may lead to a greater sense of belonging and an increased ability to lead with conviction. Conversely, if you find a mismatch between your 'moral compass' and that of your company and colleagues, self-awareness will give you the courage to act.

As well as a route to understanding identity and purpose, self-awareness is the first step towards emotional intelligence, a key trait of a successful leader. Emotional intelligence is divided into the ability to be aware of, manage and express your emotions (the Self-awareness and Self-management quadrants on the diagram below) and the capacity to understand others and to handle relationships wisely and with empathy (the Social Awareness and Relationship Management quadrants below).

Self-awareness	Social Awareness
Self-management	Relationship Management

With self-awareness comes the recognition that a gap exists between what happens and how you respond. This awareness leads to greater self-control, more choice, and the ability to shape your experiences and learn from your mistakes.

A great example of how emotional intelligence can be harnessed by a leader is Nelson Mandela. His biographer, Anthony Sampson, wrote that on being sent to jail for 27 years, he commented: 'I was made by the law a criminal, not because of what I had done but because of what I stood for', illustrating how self-awareness helped him to accept the court's decision with grace. When in jail, it was self-management that helped Mandela channel his passion for freedom into a vision for the future: 'We don't have to be victims of our past... we can let go of our bitterness, and [that] all of us can achieve greatness'. Having an awareness of yourself and an ability to control your emotions will also enable you to empathise with others and manage your relationships. As your appreciation of the similarities and differences between people grows, you will naturally become more forgiving and more adept at adapting your approach. As Mandela said: 'There were many dark moments when my faith in humanity was sorely tested, but I would not and could not give myself up to despair.[4]

Self-awareness – and the related emotional intelligence – is often what brings leaders to a great sense of wisdom, ease, assuredness and respect for others. These qualities combine to convey a sense of solidity and weight, strength, and a quiet control, all of which carry the hallmarks of leading with gravitas.

How can you become more self-aware?

There are a range of tools that you can use to increase your self-awareness, both in the workplace and independently.

Many organisations now incorporate 360 degree feedback[5] into appraisals and offer management and leadership development programmes, all of which are likely to include an element of self-reflection, performance analysis and feedback.

If you are looking to increase self-awareness independently, there is an array of books, thought papers and talks available on and off-line, which examine leadership research and philosophies, provide a benchmark for you to measure yourself against, and offer guidance on how to develop yourself further. As well as books on leadership theory, biographies and autobiographies of historical leaders can offer a fascinating insight into the experiences, beliefs, vision and behaviours of leaders from the worlds of politics, business, sport, the arts and science.

Taking the time to 'model' leaders who inspire you, in life, online and on paper, can be an extremely effective approach to exploring

....

[4] Mandela: The Authorised Biography, *Anthony Sampson* 2011.
[5] 360 degree feedback: a system whereby you, your colleagues, managers, team members and other relevant stakeholders complete a profiling questionnaire to evaluate your performance against pre-agreed performance standards.

and developing your own leadership identity and there is a chapter at the end of this book which includes guidance on how to do this.

In addition to self-study, there is a range of resources available for you to increase self-awareness. This next section provides tools to evaluate your current position – where you are now – and maximise your potential – where you want to be in the future.

Tools for evaluating your current position

Seeking feedback

When it comes to leading with gravitas, what's most important is not what you think about yourself, but how you come across to other people. To accelerate your development I encourage you to actively seek out feedback and find as many opportunities as you can to share this valuable gift with others too. Not only will this help you to evaluate your progress, it will also help you to appreciate any discrepancies between how you think you come across and how you come across in real life. As part of my *Leading With Gravitas* programmes, I often ask participants to deliver a short presentation about themselves. At the end, they will typically focus on how nervous they thought they appeared – which is rarely as bad as they think.

> Laura
>
> As Laura, one participant, noted: 'My biggest epiphany was that what people see on the outside is not necessarily what is going on inside. I feel more able now to step into people's perceptions of me, which appear to be positive, and own those.'

There are a number of ways in which you can make feedback part of your working culture. Firstly, make the time to incorporate it into meetings with colleagues, clients, customers, mentors, line managers and direct reports, being specific about the behaviour or activity you are discussing. The more you offer well-intentioned, constructive feedback, the more likely they will reciprocate and the more the whole team grows. You can also request feedback on one-off events or projects. For example, if you want to evaluate your impact in a presentation, distribute a feedback form or ask members of the audience for their views.

Another valuable technique is to build self-evaluation into your day. When a task has gone particularly well – or badly – ask yourself what was it that you did, or didn't do, that made the difference – and ensure you incorporate the learning next time. To increase awareness of how you come across, ask a colleague to video you and watch it back, paying particular attention to your voice, body language, posture and tone and looking for what you did well and what you could do to improve.

Finally, remember that feedback is a subjective gift born out of people's perception of you. This is not the time to disagree or defend, even if you don't like everything you hear. I have invariably found that when a piece of feedback is painful, I will find within it a precious gem of learning, which I would have missed if I'd brushed it aside because of a bruised ego. With all feedback, take the time to examine it, think about where the useful truth is, and work out what you'll do differently next time.

Exercise

Make a note of three ways in which you will seek feedback, and how you will use the feedback for personal development. Then look back on the feedback you've received recently that has had a bearing on your leadership and gravitas. Consider what learning you can continue to apply today – and the impact that this will have in the future.

Johari's Window

Another useful tool for increasing awareness of your current position is Johari's Window, devised in the 1950s by Joe Luft and Harry Ingham, two psychology professors at the University of California. They observed that there are aspects of our personality that we're open about, and others that we keep to ourselves. At the same time, there are traits that others see in us that we're not aware of, as well as untapped potential that is not recognised by ourselves or others. The Window is represented as a four-box grid:

1 **PUBLIC/OPEN AREA** **Known to me and others** Contains aspects of our personality that are openly known and talked about – which may be seen as strengths or weaknesses. This is the self that we choose to share with others.	2 **HIDDEN AREA** **Known to others** **but not to me** Contains character traits that others observe in us that we don't know about ourselves. Again, they could be positive or negative behaviours, and will affect the way that others perceive us and act towards us.
3 **PRIVATE AREA** **Known to me** **but not to others** Contains aspects of our self that we know about and keep hidden from others.	4 **UNKNOWN AREA** **Not acknowledged by me** **or known to others** Contains aspects of our personality that nobody knows about us – including ourselves. This may be because we don't currently access those areas, or because they're currently in our subconscious.

This tool was used by Claire, a marketing consultant who attended one of my *Leading with Gravitas* programmes to increase her gravitas and self-confidence in preparation for an important interview. In Quadrant 1 (known to me and others), she put her marketing qualifications and the companies where she'd worked. In Quadrant 2 (known to others but not to me), after reflection and feedback from the group, she put her finesse with words, her ability to light up a room, her business 'savvy'. In Quadrant 3 (known to me, but not to others), she acknowledged her astute understanding of 'what makes people tick', based in part on a coaching qualification that she had obtained a few years back. Having completed the previous quadrants, Claire realised that Quadrant 4 (not acknowledged by me or known to others) represented her passion for putting people at the heart of an organisation, which she had not had the opportunity to fulfil in previous roles. Completing Johari's Window helped Claire to appreciate that her future role would need to incorporate both her marketing expertise and her focus on people development, and that she would make this absolutely clear in her interview.

Claire

· · · · · · · · · · · · · · · ·

Exercise

· · · · · · · · · · · · · · · ·

Create your own Johari's Window as it relates to your leadership style and gravitas, taking into consideration how you see yourself and the feedback you've received from others. You can use the guide questions below to prompt your thinking.[6]

---

[6] For an online version of your Johari's Window, go to www.leadingwithgravitas.com/resources.

Quadrant 1: Public/Open: known to me and others

- What strengths and weaknesses are evident in the way you present yourself?
- What feedback do you consistently get from others?
- What do teams, clients, colleagues and customers most value in you?
- What other aspects of your personality are known both to you and others?

Quadrant 2: Hidden: known to others but not me

- What feedback have you received – from friends, family and colleagues – that has surprised you? NB: if you haven't received feedback recently, identify three or four people whose opinion you trust to share their thoughts.
- In which instances do colleagues come to you for support, and when do they go elsewhere?
- What can you do 'with your eyes closed' that others find challenging?
- What else might be known to others, but not recognised by you?

Quadrant 3: Private: known to me but not to others

- What are your hidden talents – what light do you hide 'under a bushel'?
- What areas of your life or aspects of your personality do you prefer to keep hidden from others?
- What qualities do you display at home that you don't show at work, and vice versa?
- What else might be known to you, but not to others?

Quadrant 4: Unknown: not acknowledged by me or known to others

- What do you think was the driving force that got you to where you are today?
- What future potential do you think you might hold which is yet to be revealed? For clues, consider your greatest unfulfilled passion; the pastimes you most enjoy; home interests which you could bring to work.
- What else might be not yet known to you or others?

Having filled in your Johari's Window, consider:

- Which areas of your life are currently hidden, under-exposed, or under-used which might enhance your leadership qualities and your gravitas?
- What would it be like if your Open/Known quadrant grew to incorporate the other quadrants? If what you recognised about yourself and what people knew about you were the same?
- What advice would you give to a colleague who had the same Johari's Window as you to maximise their leadership potential and gravitas?
- How will these insights inform your future development?

Tools for evaluating your future potential

Setting goals to lead with gravitas

As you become more familiar with where you are now, you will begin to consider where you want to be and your future potential. The first step in making this future vision of yourself a reality is defining your goals.

Traditional goal-setting is often linked to 'SMART' metrics, where each goal has to be Specific, Measurable, Achievable, Realistic or Relevant, and Time-bound. Although this brings with it a rigour of thinking, it can be restrictive and potential-sapping – if a goal is realistic and achievable, why aren't you doing it right now?

Many work-related goals are created with a short term outcome in mind and in response to an unsatisfactory situation: objectives might include 'to break down silos within the organisation' or 'to handle challenging conversations effectively'.

For personal development to occur on a grander scale, the secret is to broaden your thinking to encompass longer term results that make a difference not only to you, but to your wider organisation and the world. Rather than linking your goals to a present situation you don't like, as above, link them to a future situation which inspires you. Objectives devised by leaders looking to enhance their gravitas by using this 'wider' thinking might include 'to create a culture of meaningful collaboration within the organisation', 'to seek out the win/win in all team interactions', or 'to acknowledge opposing views and seek out learning opportunities in points of difference'. Notice how these objectives focus on *the solution* that you want to achieve, as opposed to *the problem* you want to get away from.

For profound change to occur, instead of limiting your goals to a set of words that you refer to once at your appraisal when they're set, and once more when you check them a year later, create goals that you can see, hear, feel and touch on a daily basis. Choose goals that get your pulse going and your heart racing and objectives that excite and inspire you. Think about what will happen as a result of achieving your goals, the impact on you, your colleagues, your loved ones. Make them so compelling that they inspire and enliven your everyday life.

Exercise

Spend some time thinking about goals that will inspire you to reach your full potential and lead with gravitas.

Now take yourself to a time in the future when you have fulfilled your potential as a leader with gravitas. Consider:

- What are people seeing in your behaviour, in your physical appearance, in the way you carry yourself?
- What are people hearing – the words you say, the way you say them? How are people responding?
- What does it feel like to be leading with gravitas? What emotions are you experiencing and how are other people feeling in your presence?

Now think about what tangible evidence will illustrate that you are leading with gravitas:

- What will be your title and role one, five, ten years from now and what results will you have delivered?
- What will your teams/colleagues/clients be saying about you as a leader?
- What awards, accolades and accomplishments will you be able to say were down to you and your team?
- What purpose will you have fulfilled as a result of reaching your goals?

Finally, think about those situations when you will be leading with gravitas and the difference you will have made in your professional and personal life.

Logical Levels of Change

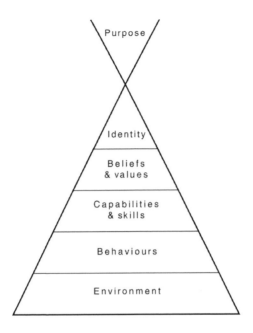

The Logical Levels of Change is another useful model for developing an understanding of how you currently think and operate at various levels and what you might like to change for the future. Developed by Robert Dilts and Todd Epstein, who were in turn inspired by Gregory Bateson and Bertrand Russell, the model is built up of six hierarchical stages: Environment, Behaviour, Capabilities and skills, Beliefs and values, Identity and Purpose.

As you consider how you embody your leadership style, you can think of your purpose as your spine or backbone, your values as your life organs, your beliefs as your brain, your capabilities as your life blood, your behaviour as the cells and your environment as the skin which surrounds you.

Exercise

Take a look at the Logical Levels diagram. As you consider your role as a leader with gravitas, reflect on each of the logical levels, starting at the bottom of the pyramid with Environment and ending at the top with Purpose. You can use the questions to guide your thinking:

1 Environment: this level refers to the physical environment around you including the people, places and objects, the tools and resources available and the culture. To gain insight into your current role and your future potential, ask yourself: How does my environment affect my goal? What are my external opportunities or barriers? What are my resources? What kind of people do I have around me? What does my physical appearance say about who I am?

2 Behaviours: this level relates to your actions and habits. To deepen your insight into the behaviours that support and hinder you, consider: What characteristic behaviours are reflective of my personality? How does my behaviour reflect my role as a leader with gravitas or hold me back? What behaviours would I like to develop to enhance my leadership and gravitas?

3 Capabilities and skills: this level reflects the abilities, talents, expertise and competencies that determine your behaviour. Consider what skills, talents and competencies you already possess that enable you to achieve the results you desire; also think about the skills and capabilities you have not yet developed to lead with gravitas.

4 Beliefs and values: beliefs and values are the forces that define who you are and determine how you live your life. They have developed over time through your upbringing and in response to experiences, and yet you may be unaware of what they are

and how they influence you. To deepen your understanding, consider the principles that steer you; the values that you hold dear, the beliefs you hold to be true and how they may be supporting you or holding you back. Consider also your beliefs and values about leadership and how they relate to your organisation's values and principles.

5 Identity: this level relates to your sense of self and your role in the world. To gain a deeper understanding of your leadership identity and how this comes across ask yourself how you define your role at work and in life. What do you stand for? How is the way you lead your life an expression of who you are? How do you see yourself and how do others see you as a leader? Consider also how you relate to your organisation's mission.

6 Purpose: this is the point at the top of the pyramid where the lines intersect and then extend outwards to the wider world. The highest logical level relates to the wider meaning in your life and the purpose you would like to fulfil. Consider what are your personal goals in life? What difference do you want to make in the world? What moves you to take action? How would you like to be remembered as a leader? What is your organisation's vision and how do you relate to that? [7]

Having completed your Logical Levels of Change pyramid, you can create a series of statements to encapsulate your 'leadership voice'. This draws together the values, beliefs, sense of identity and purpose that lie at the heart of your gravitas, the passion and vision that drive and steer you, and the energy that inspires others to follow you. These statements can be literal or metaphorical. One leader

---

[7] For an online version of your Logical Levels of Change pyramid, go to www.leadingwithgravitas.com/resources.

described himself as the conductor of an orchestra, drawing the best from each musician to create a unified sound; another used a rugby analogy, likening his role to a player always searching for the next gap; another used his voice to inspire people to choose their attitude in any given circumstance.

Once you are clear on your leadership voice, it becomes much easier to lead with conviction, to act assertively, and communicate with strength. It comes through not only in the words you use, but also the way you carry yourself, and in the way you relate to others. This is not something that will come to you in an instant, although it will become clearer the longer you reflect on the inner components of the Gravitas Wheel©.

Exercise

Take some time now to consider what your leadership voice might be. You can come back to this again once you've been through the exercises in this book.

The Gravitas Wheel©

The Gravitas Wheel© is a unique tool for assessing, developing and monitoring your leadership and gravitas. If you have not yet done so, fill in the Gravitas Wheel© that you'll find towards the beginning of this chapter or go to the *Leading with Gravitas* website for an online version. This will help you to identify your inner and outer strengths and areas for development and therefore prioritise the chapters in this book.

Using self-awareness to build confidence

A common approach that people take when looking to build self-awareness is to identify elements of themselves which they would like to change because they are in some way unsatisfactory. It's as though we're hard-wired as human beings to seek out the negative, and ignore or discredit the positive.

In doing this we can become our own worst enemies. Instead of acknowledging and celebrating what has gone well, we focus on what has gone 'badly', building an ongoing and steady stream of criticism that we direct towards ourselves: 'That was stupid; I can't believe I said that!'; 'Why would they choose me?' or 'What must they think of me now?' These voices are in all of us, and they have the potential to take over our heads completely, especially when we are tired, under pressure or facing challenging times.

Another barrier to confidence can be competitiveness, where we compare ourselves to others – usually unfavourably – and begin to see them as a threat. Although competition can be healthy between teams, it can often be detrimental between individuals. As we look over our shoulder at how other people are doing, we can come across as self-centred, insecure and petty, and lose focus on our own purpose or the job in hand.

One of the most effective routes to building self-confidence is to identify what input you need to feel good about yourself. You could think of it like a magnet. You can choose to fire up a negatively-charged force that attracts self-doubt, criticism and all the evidence of things that have 'gone wrong'. Or you could choose to fire up a positively-charged magnet that attracts confidence, recognition, praise and self-worth. In choosing to fire up the positive magnet you not only enhance the way that you think about yourself, you are also creating a virtuous cycle mindset that's conducive to ongoing success.

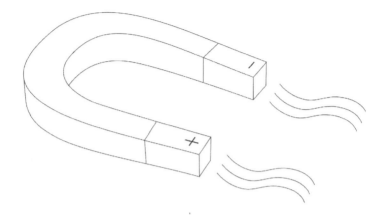

People tend to be either 'internally referenced', i.e., they need to create evidence for themselves of a job well done, or 'externally referenced', i.e., they need recognition from others. If internal validation makes you tick, train your brain to focus on what you've done well rather than what you could have done better. For external validation, make feedback part of your working culture – with the secret being to make sure you absorb the positive qualities as well as what you could do to improve.

John

A few years ago I worked with John, a site manager at a construction company, who wanted to build his confidence when liaising with senior colleagues and enhance his gravitas during weekly team meetings. John realised that when preparing for these meetings he would replay in his mind all those times when he had felt belittled by colleagues, and imagine the multitude of ways in which they would criticise him in the future. To break this cycle of negative thinking, John decided to spend half an hour a week identifying three contributions he had made in the past week and three ways he would communicate these in the next meeting. In time, John noticed that colleagues related to him in a more supportive and inclusive way, and that the trepidation he felt had been replaced with positive expectation around how his updates would be received.

John

An effective technique to encourage positive thinking is to write a journal in which you record all the results you're proud of and occasions when you've pushed yourself to achieve your full potential. Deliberately recalling examples when you've done well will boost your confidence on a daily basis. Replaying them in your mind as you prepare for challenges will inspire you to deliver your best.

Exercise

Make a note of three scenarios from the past year which illustrated your leadership and three situations when you demonstrated gravitas.

Overcoming challenges

Although increasing self-awareness will help you to pay due attention to your positive qualities, you may also find that this level of introspection may unveil aspects that you may find uncomfortable. As you take the time to look in the mirror and ask others to share what they see, you may not always be happy with what is reflected back.

Key to self-awareness is the knowledge that you are in charge of how deeply you explore your own mind and how you respond to what you find out. From working through the tools in this book, to seeking feedback, to examining your own behaviours and beliefs, remember that you are in charge, that you can work at the level you feel comfortable, and that through self-awareness comes the possibility of change.

There is a range of services that you can access to support you on your journey, from seeking the support of a trusted work colleague, friend or family member, to signing up to a training or personal development course, to booking a session with a qualified coach or counsellor. Awareness is power, and by identifying areas of strength and areas of current weakness, you will be actively moving towards your future potential.

Chapter 2

Expertise

'Follow an expert.'

• Virgil •

Expertise is the second segment of the Gravitas Wheel©, an inner quality that sits between *Self-awareness* and *Authenticity*. Expertise is a crucial ingredient for leaders with gravitas: the substance that underpins their authority, the evidence that illustrates their right to their position, and the building block that got them to where they are today. In a competitive work environment, expertise and results are the tangible measures that people use to rate you as a leader.

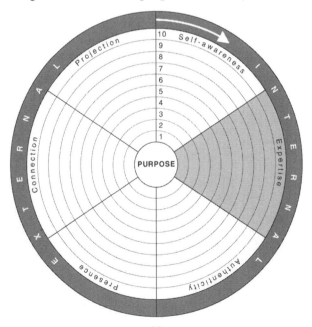

Although it's possible to convey an air of gravitas through passion and flair, over time, unless you have solid expertise under your belt, you may find yourself exposed and lose credibility. When it comes to career progression, those who demonstrate expertise will be more likely to receive recognition than those who expect their work to speak for itself. Leaders who share their expertise widely and generously are respected, trusted and admired. However, leaders who over-play their expertise can be perceived as arrogant, a trait which may detract from their gravitas. Wear your experience well – but wear it lightly.

To build gravitas, what's important is acknowledging the value that your expertise brings and finding ways for it to be appreciated by others. Expertise is a tool, a means to an end, which comes into its own when combined with your unique qualities and purpose in life. If you want to differentiate yourself from your peers it's important to acknowledge and articulate not only the qualifications and career history that are on your CV, but also the qualities that you – and only you – bring to the role.

What is expertise, and how can you use it to lead with gravitas?

The dictionary definition of the word 'expert' is 'a person who is very knowledgeable about or skilful in a particular area'. Expertise comes in different forms and can be technical, intellectual, scientific, creative, or, most likely, a blend of the above. Yet expertise in isolation is a sterile state that is only truly brought alive through the lens of personal experience and the wisdom of years.

For a leader to be perceived as an expert, their approach should bring together a combination of knowledge (the theoretical or practical understanding of a subject), experience (practical contact with and observation of facts or events) and dedication to a particular field.

This combined requirement for knowledge and experience is eloquently illustrated in a story shared by Mike, an HR director, who interviewed two candidates for a leadership position, both of whom had equivalent qualifications and career histories. The first talked at length about their technical expertise and the results they'd delivered throughout their career. Their communication style was dry, factual and matter-of-fact. The second peppered their career history with anecdotes about the people they'd worked with and lessons they'd learned along the way. They spoke with passion about their vision for the prospective company and their personal leadership phi-losophy. The interviewer concluded that although the first candidate would be suited to a project management role, it was the second who had the qualities they required in a leader.

As well as bringing together knowledge and experience, true expertise is attained through many years in a chosen field. Malcolm Gladwell, in his book *Outliers*, quotes a study by Anders Ericsson, which estimated that it takes 10,000 hours to reach a level of 'greatness'. While you may need to put the hours in to become a world-renowned expert, it is possible to be seen as an expert after a relatively short space of time if you have a perspective that's valued by others. Expertise is relative – a teacher may only need to be a few stages ahead of their pupils to impart useful information – and continually evolving. Even those at the top of their profession need to keep up with latest advances to maintain their position.

How does expertise come across?

Expertise is revealed in a person's confidence in their subject matter, their encyclopaedic breadth and depth of knowledge, their ability to draw information from a variety of sources and their finesse in joining up the dots in a persuasive way. People with expertise tend to display a passion for their topic, which comes across in their energy, focus and drive. When you observe an expert talking about their subject, they use a direct communication style, whether citing facts or sharing personal opinion, choosing the definitive 'I believe...', rather than the more open-ended 'I think...'

You can also tell an expert through their demeanour, which is typically level-headed, rational and grounded. As they perform their role they are often swan-like above the water, appearing focused, competent and in control, even though their legs may be paddling furiously underwater. When facing a challenge or problem, they don't flap. Their reaction is reflexive, almost instinctive, and they remain calm in the face of a crisis. When you are in their presence you feel safe, you trust that they will not let you down, and you relax in the knowledge that they will provide sound counsel and get the job done – all of which goes a long way to conveying gravitas.

Defining your expertise

If you're looking to build your expertise as a route to gravitas, the good news is that the other elements of the Gravitas Wheel© will help you. *Self-awareness* will give you confidence in the knowledge and experience you possess, *Authenticity* and *Presence* will enable you to share your personal interpretation of knowledge in an engaging way, and *Connection* and *Projection* will help you to transmit your expertise to a variety of audiences.

The first step in developing expertise is to identify which area, or niche, you would like to represent. Although it may feel safer to develop your skills widely, the higher up you go, the more associating yourself with a defined area will help to differentiate you and the more time you will have to deepen your knowledge and experience.

Begin by considering in what ways you are, or could be, an expert. Think about your professional qualifications, career history, personal qualities, as well as what you enjoy doing and those areas of your business, organisation or sector which require a level of expertise to stand out. Consider also how your expertise comes across: what do people see, hear and feel when you are talking about your area of expertise? What impact would you like your expertise to have, now and in the future? Reflect also on how your expertise defines you as a leader, how it helps to fulfil your company's vision and mission and what impact you would like it to have on the wider world.

An effective tool for evaluating expertise is the SWOT as it enables you to assess your *internal* Strengths and Weaknesses and the *external* Opportunities and Threats that could support and hinder your development.[8]

---

[8] For an online verson of your SWOT, go to www.leadingwithgravitas.com/resources.

Exercise

Complete your own SWOT as it relates to your expertise, using the guiding questions to help you.

Strengths: internal traits that propel you forward	Weaknesses: internal traits that hold you back
In which areas do you excel or stand out as an expert?	In which areas are you currently lacking as an expert?
What skills, qualifications and experience qualify and differentiate you as an expert?	What gaps do you currently have in your skills set, qualifications and experience?
In which areas of your job do you consistently receive positive feedback?	In which areas of your job do you consistently receive negative feedback?
Opportunities: external factors that could support you	**Threats: external factors that could hinder you**
What unmet needs could you fulfil in your company/sector through your expertise?	What obstacles do you face that could prevent you from sharing your expertise?
What changes are occurring in your industry and how can you take advantage of them?	How might your role/company/sector be changing in ways that don't match your expertise?
What internal/external opportunities exist for you to raise your profile as an expert?	What internal/external factors exist that could threaten your position as an expert?
What skills and experience could you acquire to develop your expertise further?	What barriers might there be that block your development as an expert?
How can your network support you in achieving your goals?	Are any colleagues competing with you for work or roles?

Once you have completed your SWOT, consider the following questions as they relate to your leadership position and gravitas:

- Which area or niche would you like to represent as an expert?
- Which are your key strengths and how will you capitalise on them?
- Which are your key weaknesses and how will you address them?
- Which are the key threats that you need to mitigate?
- Which are the key opportunities that you can harness?

Once you have identified the area of expertise you'd like to be known for, the next step is to hone your capabilities so that you can make a real difference and stand out from the crowd. Whereas the temptation may be to reach a certain level of expertise and stop there, advice from people at the top of their profession advocates an ongoing receptiveness to ideas and a willingness to seek fresh perspectives.

Just like all the other components of the Gravitas Wheel©, expertise is a constantly evolving state, which you can actively develop and add your own twist to over time.

Luke Dale Roberts

Luke Dale Roberts, entrepreneur and number one chef in South Africa, put the drive for ongoing self-development this way: 'True expertise is knowing as much as you can about a particular topic and practising until it comes naturally to you. I've listened, paid attention to what I've been taught and tried to execute everything perfectly. It's then about applying your own method or theory to enhance it further. If you don't add your personal interpretation then you're simply regurgitating what has come before'.

To accelerate your expertise:

1 Begin by finding your niche. Identify an area you're passionate about and that you know you will excel in, now and in the future.

2 Expand on your professional qualifications through professional development, on-the-job training and CPD (continuing professional development).

3 Take responsibility for projects that will make best use of your expertise and allow you to develop further in that area.

4 Keep your knowledge current by reading journals, newspapers and magazines, as well as attending symposia, conferences, events and exhibitions. Ensure you not only take in information, but also develop your own point of view to share.

5 Model experts, both in your chosen field and those you admire generally: examine how their expertise has evolved, how they communicate, and what they do to keep their expertise current (for guidance on how to model expertise, turn to chapter 7).

....
Exercise
....

Make a note of the steps you will take to accelerate your expertise, when these steps will be completed and how you will measure progress.

Raising your profile as an expert

Although you may feel like your expertise should speak for itself, in a busy and competitive work environment the combination of hard work and modesty is unlikely to get you the recognition you need to achieve your goals. The need to 'do your own PR' is becoming increasingly relevant for leaders who want to progress, as it's what will differentiate you and get you onto the radar for more senior positions.

A key part of building your reputation as an expert is the ability to raise your profile in a way that doesn't look like bragging, especially in cultures where it's perceived to be self-indulgent or even arrogant to do so.

Ensure your title reflects your expertise and, if you have any letters after your name, make sure to use them, in email signatures, business cards and correspondence.

Identify which projects you would like to lead, which committees and teams you would like to be part of and which opinions and values you would like to be known for. Offer to mentor or coach people within your organisation and externally. Sharing your expertise in this way will help you to appreciate the value you bring and illustrate your worth more widely than your immediate circle.

The way you look will also affect the way you're perceived. Take a look at how experts in your organisation and sector dress, think about whether you want to conform to or rebel against that style and adapt your image accordingly. If you would like to appear more experienced than your age you may choose to adopt a conservative style or 'dress for the position you're heading for rather than the position you're in', as advised by a VP in an international bank. On the other hand, if you're looking to appear approachable and engaging, you may choose more casual attire, along the lines of Sir Richard Branson and the late Steve Jobs, paying close attention to the quality, provenance and cut.

In addition to raising your profile in your own workplace, it's important to consider how you will elevate your status in the wider business community. Grow your network by joining professional organisations associated with your area of expertise. Attend events and build relationships with people who appreciate your skills and will speak positively about you to their own contacts. To set yourself apart from other experts in your field, develop a unique point of view to share through speaker engagements, articles, blogs and books as well as online through professional and social networks associated with your sector.

Communicating expertise with gravitas

Having raised your profile as an expert, it's vital that you can talk about your specialist skills and experience engagingly. Many experts are highly proficient in their field, but struggle expressing themselves in public, whether introducing themselves, talking about their subject or delivering a presentation.

In working with leaders on developing their expertise, I've noticed that what sometimes affects confidence is the belief that you have to know everything about a subject before you have the right to talk about it. In fact, what's important for your audience is your ability to separate the 'must knows' from the 'nice to knows' and making your knowledge relevant. If you want to convey confidence and authority, whether in a presentation, job interview or leading a team, don't try to become an expert on the whole subject: focus instead on your particular slice of expertise and the value it brings to your audience, and talk about that.

Jennifer Simmons

Jennifer Simmons runs a successful marketing company which is regularly invited to present ideas to prospective clients. Her advice is: 'When pitching for business, the temptation is to try to become an expert overnight. This is never going to happen. Although our clients will certainly have more knowledge of their products than us, they are coming to us for our recommendations on how to market those products, and we are the experts on that.'

Developing an 'elevator pitch'

The following steps have been designed to help you to answer the dreaded 'what do you do?' question, whether networking, being interviewed, meeting new colleagues, or, literally, in an elevator. You will also be able to use these words and phrases, either out loud or in your head, to give you focus and boost confidence in situations where you want to present your best self.[9]

1 Start by asking yourself 'who are my audiences and how do I want to come across to them?' These may include current/future employers, customers/clients, colleagues and peer groups.

2 Now create a table like the one below and note down the words you could use to describe yourself to these audiences:

Skills & Capabilities	Personal Qualities	Results Delivered	Impact
e.g.: strategic, creative, collaborative, innovative, specialist in…	e.g.: calm, dynamic, inspirational, empathetic, driven, independent, entrepreneurial	e.g.: innovative solutions, award-winning, sales growth, skills development	e.g.: people development, cultural change, market leadership, personal growth

[9] To complete this exercise online, go to www.leadingwithgravitas.com/resources.

3   Then, taking each of your audiences in turn, circle the words in your table that are most relevant to them. For example, for your company board, skills and capabilities might include 'strategic, commercially astute', qualities might include 'reliable, results-orientated', results might include 'targets in X' or 'Y percent growth' and impact might include 'uniquely differentiated, delighted shareholders'.

4   Then, using the words you've circled, create up to three sentences to describe yourself, combining your skills and capabilities, personal qualities, results and impact. You may like to tailor each of your sentences to the audiences you mostly come into contact with. For example, 'I combine my [insert skills and capabilities] with my [insert personal qualities] to create [insert results] that [insert impact]'.

NB: Please don't feel like you need to follow this formula to the letter. What's important is creating a set of words that describe you in a way that feels comfortable and realistic. As you work through this exercise, you may come up with more words and phrases that are more relevant to you and your audiences. Make sure you capture these as you go.

5   Once you have a series of sentences you're happy with, test them out with colleagues and friends to check that they describe the real you and get the response you're looking for. If they sound too much like an advertising slogan, or you feel self-conscious saying them, try tweaking the wording and content until you are satisfied.

6   Finally, make sure you use these phrases regularly and bear in mind that, as you develop and come into contact with new audiences, you may want to evolve your phrases accordingly.

Show not tell

As well as knowing how to introduce yourself, it's important to know how to talk about your accomplishments in a way that subtly raises your profile without sounding like blatant self-aggrandisement. Instead of indiscriminately peppering your conversations with information about you, the art of 'show not tell' is when you share insights which you think are likely to be relevant and illustrate your capabilities with examples that make your expertise come alive.

James Jackson, Director at a media agency, recommends the following dos and don'ts: 'What people find annoying are those 'all-staffer' emails where people share the details of their latest successes to everyone in the company. A smarter approach is to target specific information to those teams who will find it most useful. That way they get some meaningful insights and you get the recognition for your work.'

Careful selection of the words 'I' and 'we' will also influence the way that people perceive your expertise. Senior leaders with gravitas have often reached a point where they no longer have to emphasize their personal achievements and prefer to place the emphasis on the team. On the other hand, an emerging leader may want to *personally* associate themselves with results to stand out.

Compare the following 'I' and 'we' statements:
- *'I' statement:* 'I head up the mergers division, have recently taken on responsibility for the company's diversity initiative, am in charge of a team of 50 people and delivered £20k savings last year.'
- *'We' statement:* 'Last year, my team devised an innovative model to analyse cost savings across the company. As well as recovering £20k in lost revenue, we shared the model with two other divisions, which contributed to the organisation's overall profitability and supported the work that we're doing on quality and standardisation.'

Both of these statements are talking about the same year, the same team and the same results. Each says a lot about the person speaking. And each will trigger a very different response.

Presenting your expertise

As well as knowing how to talk about your accomplishments, it's important to cultivate a presentation style that conveys expertise and gravitas. Although the most effective communicators seem to share their expertise spontaneously, what appears to be a natural style has often been carefully honed over time.

When opening a talk, the first step to engaging your audience is demonstrating your right to be at the front of the room, unless of course you're so well-respected that you need no introduction. An elegant way to do this that avoids blowing your own trumpet is asking someone else to introduce you. If this isn't an option, when you step up, after saying 'hello', make sure you mention not only who you are, your title and where you're from, but also share a little about your personal 'take' on the subject matter, so that people see the personality behind the expertise.

If you are still in the process of building your profile as an expert, a useful technique is to borrow the badge of authority from others. You can do this by citing perspectives and research conducted by other thought leaders (giving credit where credit's due) and talking about well-known colleagues from your professional circle. In doing this, you will naturally become associated with that peer group and your status will begin to rise accordingly.

When planning your presentation, an effective strategy is thinking about what you would like to achieve as a result of your talk, who your audience is and therefore what you're going to say. Questions to ask yourself include:

1 On a scale of 1 to 10, what is their level of knowledge and interest in the topic I'll be covering and how can I ensure that my material is tailored to that level?

2 What key facts and messages would I like to communicate, how much time do I have and what can I realistically cover?

3 How would I like my audience to feel as a result of my talk? Depending on your objectives and subject matter, you may want them to be inspired, relieved, curious, concerned or enthralled, all of which will require a different approach from you.

4 What latest findings, concepts and nuggets can I share that they won't get from anyone else?

5 If I'm going to be covering some dry and technical material, how can I make it interesting and relevant? You could consider showing images, distributing props or sharing case studies and anecdotes to enliven the data.

A concern that many expert speakers express is the need to communicate complex information in a format that's accessible and absorbing, without being patronising or 'dumbing down'. The most compelling experts are those who can take dry, technical and complicated information and communicate it in a language that everyone can understand. Examples include Sir David Attenborough and Stephen Hawking, who have brought elaborate concepts onto our television screens through their passion and finesse with language, fascinating us in the process.

Although the temptation may be to illustrate one's expertise by providing as much information as possible, the dual keys to an engaging talk are firstly, simplicity, and secondly, 'less is more'. Although it may be tempting to use buzz words as shorthand or to demonstrate your knowledge of a shared language, it's worth bearing in mind that, in a world full of techno-babble, acronyms and sound bites, people with the greatest gravitas are often those who are able to rise above the jargon and use plain English.

Another effective technique is to decide that your audience is capable of understanding complicated information, and then stating that belief out loud. For example, 'I'm going to introduce you to some complex concepts here. However, with your level of interest and experience, I'm sure you'll pick them up in no time.' This approach illustrates a sense of confidence in the audience and a willingness to open their minds to the new information.

Expertise in conversation

As well as demonstrating your expertise in planned settings, you will also want to illustrate your knowledge in less formal situations where you'll have less control over what topics come up. Although it may be tempting to gloss over subjects you're unsure of or pretend to know more than you do, this can be a dangerous ploy and leave you feeling quite exposed if you're found out. Ensure that any factual claims you make are backed up by evidence – use the mantra 'if you can't prove it, don't use it' – and if you don't know the answer to a question, be honest and commit to providing the answer when you have it.

Although it may sound counterintuitive, expertise is evident as much through the questions you ask as what you say. Asking precise questions that are directly relevant to the field you operate in will illustrate that you know what you're talking about, and can 'talk the same language' as the other person.

Finally, in raising your profile as an expert, it's worth noting that, as Benjamin Franklin said: 'It takes many good deeds to build a good reputation, and only one bad one to lose it.' Particularly in a digital environment where, more than ever, 'a lie travels halfway around the world while the truth is putting on its shoes' (Mark Twain), it's important to remember that any gossip or flaws in your professional reputation, whether founded or not, could stick with you far longer than any positive attributes.

Although it may be tempting, in a competitive environment, to critique others' work, remember that even with the best intentions, whatever you say and do – on or offline – could be misconstrued and will influence the way you're perceived. Treat others with the respect that you would like to receive, even if you may not always value or agree with their views and ensure that everything you say and do reflects the professionalism for which you would like to be known.

Exercise

- Make a note of three situations coming up where you would like to demonstrate your expertise.
- Outline three techniques you will use to communicate your expertise in a credible, relevant and engaging way.

Although expertise alone is not enough to convey gravitas, it does provide the backbone, or evidence to underpin it. The world's greatest leaders have gone down in history because they have combined their knowledge and life experience with a desire to fulfil a purpose that goes beyond personal gain. In doing so, they have applied their expertise to a long term vision, related their role to a global cause, honed and trusted their instinct and demonstrated courage, conviction and imagination along the way. As you develop your expertise as a leader with gravitas, consider the impact that you want your knowledge and experience to have on the world beyond your role, and the difference that you will make to the world through sharing it.

Chapter 3

Authenticity

*'The privilege of a lifetime is
to become who you truly are.'*

• C G Jung •

Authenticity is a key component of the Gravitas Wheel©, an inner quality which comes after *Self-awareness* and *Expertise*. Leaders with gravitas have authenticity at their core. They have come to know themselves, warts and all, and have found the strength of character to let themselves be seen. They have learnt to harness their authenticity

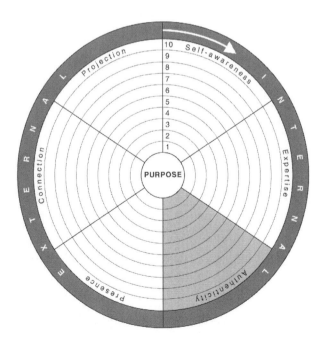

in a way that is true to their inner selves, while adapting to the various audiences and circumstances in which they find themselves.

Authenticity may at first appear to be the easiest nut to crack on the Gravitas Wheel©, yet it can be the hardest one to get right in the workplace, where people are expecting you to behave in a certain way. Many of my coaching clients talk about the desire to fit in: the temptation and pressure to emulate the style and behaviour of people in senior positions as a way of becoming part of the company culture. It is human nature to want to merge with 'the pack' and adapt to different environments to avoid standing out. However, what both emerging and established leaders have shared with me is that the pressure to wear various masks at work, at home and with different people can be quite exhausting, with the result being that they can start to "lose" their real self and even feel "fake" in certain circumstances. And what happens when you've striven your whole career to fit in, and then suddenly are required to differentiate yourself in order to get the next promotion, qualify for a leadership role or branch out on your own, all of which may call into question, 'who am I, how do I present my best self and how do I show up authentically?'

Authenticity has become a buzz word for the 21st century, with everything from authentic food to authentic holidays, and 7,796 books appearing on Amazon's 'authenticity books' list.[10] The term 'authentic leadership' emerged in the 1960s, calling for leaders to develop their self-identity and be true to their values as a way of engaging followers and increasing individual and team performance.

So what are the benefits of being an authentic leader today, how does authenticity contribute to gravitas, and how can you develop authenticity in a working environment where the norm may be to conform?

---

[10] Search carried out on Amazon on 26th September 2014 with the words 'authenticity books' in the search engine.

In a world governed by social media, where people create virtual identities that are an exaggeratedly polished version of themselves and post updates of impossibly perfect lives, it is refreshing to come across people who are unashamedly real. We are drawn to them because of their fallibilities and warmed by their honesty. We trust them, because in having the guts to show their true nature, rather than covering it up, they send out a clear message that they have nothing to hide.

When it comes to leading with gravitas, being authentic has a number of advantages. Allowing your real personality to be seen, particularly when steered by a clear purpose and values, will give you a groundedness and weight which will directly contribute to your gravitas. You will become less guarded, free to react spontaneously and express your views, without second-guessing whether you are saying the 'right' thing.

When you 'show up' as your authentic self, people will be more open to what you have to say, whether they agree with you or not. You will experience a natural connection and build rapport more easily and quickly. Your willingness to reveal your inner personality will give others permission to do the same, leading to a more honest and open environment that everyone will want to be part of. People will feel comfortable and safe in your presence. They will listen, respect and follow where you go. By bringing your 'whole' self to work, you will have access to a wider range of insights, perspectives and communication styles than if you simply relied on your 'work self'. This will make you more open to inspiration, leading to greater creativity and a wider spectrum of solutions.

The advantages of bringing your 'whole' self to work were experienced by Sereena, who had been passed over for promotion a couple of times, despite being fully qualified for the role. Feedback from her manager was that she didn't stand out as a candidate and that she would need to bring 'more personality' to her role. This was a challenge for Sereena, who preferred to keep her head down, save fun for the weekends, and concentrate on the job in hand rather than building relationships with colleagues.

Rather than trying to create a whole new personality for herself at work, which would have been inauthentic and extremely tiring to maintain, Sereena decided to bring aspects of her personality, which she previously expressed only at home, into the workplace. Firstly, she brought more of her nurturing qualities, previously reserved for family life, into her interactions with her team. She took responsibility for the graduate on-boarding scheme and spent more time coaching her team than previously. Secondly, she incorporated the creativity she usually applied to DIY projects at home into the design and delivery of presentations. As a result Sereena found she was more able to make connections and became known for a wider skills set, both of which contributed to the promotion she received the following year.

Sereena

What is authenticity?

The dictionary definition of 'authentic' is someone or something trustworthy and real: not fake or copied. Authentic brands do what they say on the tin and have built up a reputation of not manipulating or misleading their audiences just to make a sale.

Authenticity in the workplace resides in the fine balance between expressing who you are, daring to be different, and respecting your company culture and colleagues. For leaders wishing to make an impact, authenticity is a quality that at times may need to be reined in to be effective. Be yourself, yes, but be mindful of the consequences of sharing the lurid details of your love life at the water cooler.

This isn't about wearing your heart on your sleeve 24/7. It's about being secure in the knowledge that you are in an environment where you are valued for who *you* are as well as what you do – and letting that be seen. It's about being clear on how your principles chime with the values of your organisation – and being confident enough to share these. It's about knowing when and how to make a stand for what you believe in, in a way that is appropriate to your organisation and brings people with you, rather than alienating or putting them off.

When it comes to building gravitas, it is the combination of authenticity with the other elements of the Gravitas Wheel© which will give you impact and influence. Without *Self-awareness*, you could authentically be crashing around like a bull in a china-shop. Without *Connection*, you could authentically be upsetting people through your no-holds-barred communication style. Without *Expertise*, *Presence* or *Projection*, your authenticity could be perceived as naiveté, self-obsession or showing off: all ego-led traits which will do little for your gravitas.

Authenticity can be an extremely powerful quality and so it's important to check your motivations before revealing it, both in work and out. History is too full of unscrupulous leaders, authentically aligned to a corrupt value system, driven by authentically held, but misguided beliefs. Organisations are too full of manipulative empire-builders and ego-driven power junkies who get away with underhand behaviour, using their authenticity for personal gain. Without integrity and the Purpose that lies at the centre of the wheel, authenticity could be at worst, damaging, and at best, a waste of everyone's time.

Understanding what authenticity means for you

If you are looking to reveal more of your authentic self as a route to gravitas, the first step is understanding what the term means to you and how you would like it to come across in your leadership style.

···················
Exercise
···················

Begin by exploring what the term 'authenticity' means to you:
* What is your personal definition of authenticity?
* How do leaders you admire come across when they are being authentic?
* What are the advantages of presenting your authentic self at work?
* If you were to identify five words to describe your authentic self, what would they be? NB: you will refer back to these words later in the chapter, so pick words you think will give you a real insight into your authentic self.

Next examine how authenticity feels for you by recalling circumstances when you have felt both authentic and inauthentic:

- I have felt authentic at work when... e.g. discussing a cause you feel passionate about, briefing a team on a project you strongly believe in, outlining ideas for a new project.
- I have felt inauthentic at work when... e.g. pretending to listen to someone talking about a subject that bores you, delivering a presentation about a topic you know little about, feeling under pressure to conceal your views.

Now consider how you would like your authentic self to appear at work, how you would like to feel in those circumstances and the impact you would like to have. You may like to think of leaders you admire to aid your thinking.

- I would like my authentic self to be seen at work when... e.g. introducing yourself to new clients or colleagues, chairing a meeting, delivering a presentation.
- When being authentic at work, I would like to feel... e.g. confident, relaxed, clear-headed.
- The impact of revealing my authentic self at work will be... e.g. more spontaneity, a freedom to express myself honestly, greater rapport with colleagues, increased respect from teams.

Developing your 'best self'

Having established how you would like your authenticity to come across at work and the benefits this will bring, you can explore the practical steps you can take to make this happen. A key part of developing authenticity is having sufficient self-awareness to know who you are and liking yourself enough to feel comfortable revealing yourself. Authentic leaders do what they say on the tin, because they know what's in the tin and are content with its shade.

As well as understanding what authenticity feels like at a surface level (identified through the questions above), it's important to examine what your authenticity represents at a deeper level. Taking the time to understand your purpose, identity, values and beliefs, explored in the *Self-awareness* chapter of this book, will help you to understand the foundation of your authentic self and the building blocks of your gravitas. As a result of having this moral compass, you will find it easier to make decisions, stand up for what you believe in and react to situations consistently.

As you begin to explore your authenticity you will discover that it is not a static state, but continuously evolving, shaped by events and how you choose to respond. Authenticity not only reflects who you are today, but also who you will become tomorrow: we are not the person we were five years ago, nor the person we will be in five years' time. An analogy for this evolutionary process is the acorn, which starts out as a small, green kernel, but holds within it the DNA of a strong, stately oak tree. The only way for the acorn to become the oak tree is by becoming something that it is not, from acorn, to shoot, to sapling, to tree. So with your authenticity and gravitas.

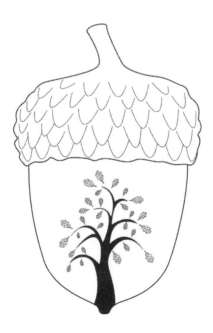

Rather than letting this process take care of itself, the most effective leaders prioritise self-development in order to cultivate what I call their 'best self': you, but you on a very good day. Central to this process is putting yourself in situations where you are out of your comfort zone, when, paradoxically, you may not feel like your authentic self at all.

The most effective route to reaching your potential is by challenging yourself, putting yourself into unfamiliar situations where you have to 'act' as if you belong there. In time, you will get to a point where you feel comfortable, safe *and* authentic. You will then be ready to move onto the next phase.

If in the process of looking in the mirror you identify aspects of your authentic self which fall short of the ideal, rather than using the excuse that you're just being yourself, consider how and what you might like to change: "being authentic" should not be an excuse for inappropriate behaviour that detracts from your gravitas.

Enlist support from a friend or colleague who can help you to identify what you're doing, saying, feeling and thinking when you're being your best authentic self, and the impact it has on others. You can then reflect on those times when you have not been satisfied with your authentic, unguarded behaviour – or when being yourself has resulted in an unsatisfactory outcome – and consider what behaviours would have been more appropriate. When you find yourself in similar situations, your self-awareness will allow you to step back and consider how your best authentic self would respond, and then take action.

By committing to personal development, the gap between your ideal authentic self and your real authentic self will narrow. In time, you will reach a state of alignment and the question of being authentic or not will lose its significance as it will simply be who you are when you show up in the world.

Exercise

Spend some time thinking about how you would like your best authentic self to emerge and how this will contribute to your overall gravitas. Consider also how you can put yourself into situations which will push you beyond your comfort zone and enable you to develop your authentic self further.

Sharing your authenticity at work

Having increased your understanding of what authenticity means for you personally, you will now be in a position to consider how freely you can express your authentic self in the workplace. For gravitas to emerge it's important to find an avenue where you can be yourself and where your beliefs and values can be realised. They are the expression of your most authentic self, central to your purpose, and a tragedy if submerged.

Jason
> Feeling compromised or stifled at work can be stressful, particularly when it feels like your values are being trampled on or you feel unable to express your views. This challenge was experienced by Jason, Creative Director at a large advertising agency, who set great store by creative freedom and felt constricted by the demands placed on him from their conservative clients. After two years of feeling compromised, Jason moved to head up a smaller agency where he was able to express his creative side and be more confident revealing his authentic self.

Another example is Jane, Head of Marketing for a restaurant chain. Although she knew her skills and capabilities were perfectly suited, she felt unfulfilled in her role and thought there was more her company could be doing to contribute to the local community. After an open discussion with her boss, Jane was given the opportunity to launch an initiative that encouraged diners to contribute a percentage of their bill to a homeless charity. This not only gave Jane a more profound sense of job satisfaction, but also created much needed funds for the charity and a boost to the restaurant whose clientele appreciated the opportunity to contribute to a worthwhile cause.

Jane

....
Exercise
....

- Reflect on the extent to which your values align with those of your organisation.
- Consider opportunities where you could express your values more widely at work, and the impact of this on you, your colleagues and the business.
- Consider how else you could express and develop your values outside the workplace, and the impact this will have on your authenticity and gravitas.

Managed authenticity and leadership 'hats'

The next step after building self-awareness is choosing how you would like your authentic self to show up at work. People who are authentic have a clear and consistent personality. They don't try to be someone they're not, or hide behind a façade of perfection. For them, staying true to their principles is more important than looking good or being nice, and so they will not shy from challenging the status quo, even if it means they lose out on the popularity ratings.

While it's important to be consistent and act with integrity, it's equally important to know how to adapt your behaviour to suit different situations, audiences and environments. Just as you would have a different conversation with your partner over dinner than with your children over tea, in the workplace you will build more lasting relationships and have a more positive impact if you modify your style when communicating with clients, colleagues, line reports or suppliers.

'Managed authenticity' is a term that I share as part of my *Leading with Gravitas* programme to take into account this very need for adaptability. Just as Einstein's definition of insanity is doing the same thing over and over and expecting different results, so, if your authentic self isn't getting the results you need, it is possible to change your behaviour while still holding onto what makes you 'you'.

In observing and profiling the most effective leaders, I've noticed that they access a variety of leadership styles, or hats, to get the results they need in different situations, while ensuring that their authentic voice and personality remain present throughout.

The types of 'hats' worn on any given day may include the visionary hat, worn to rally a team around a common goal; the commandeering hat, donned to ensure a task is performed exactly as specified; the conciliatory hat, chosen to ensure every colleague has a voice around the table; and the coach hat, selected to draw the best out of individuals and encourage growth, autonomy and resourcefulness.

As you imagine yourself putting on these hats you will realise that each comes with its own communication style and behaviours, triggering very different responses and results. In a crisis, where rapid action is required, the last hat you would pick up would be the conciliatory hat. People want action, not a discussion. At the start of a new year, where teams are looking for inspiration and direction, you wouldn't reach for the commandeering hat. People don't want to be 'told' what to think, so the visionary hat may be the best choice.

....
Exercise
....

Create a table using the headings below to identify which leadership hats you will use to be effective in various situations, how you will adapt your behaviour and communication style to suit each situation and how your authentic personality will continue to come through[11].

Situation	Leadership 'hat'	How I will adapt my behaviour to this situation	How I will adapt my communication style to this situation	How my authentic self will continue to come through

Once you have identified the various leadership hats available to you, you may wonder how to choose the most appropriate style. Since this is entirely dependent on the situation and the people, the key is to make sure you are fully 'present', which we will explore fully in the *Presence* chapter. Presence in this context is being in the room,

---

[11] To complete this exercise online, go to www.leadingwithgravitas.com/resources.

with the people, connected to what's happening here and now, rather than absorbed by your own thoughts, worrying about the past or thinking about the future. Being present will enable you to carefully observe and listen to what's really going on, step back and choose your response, before taking action.

How does authentic communication come across?

The most tangible illustration of authenticity is how a person communicates. You may have had the misfortune to meet inauthentic salespeople or individuals who seem genuine on the surface, but for some reason just don't add up. You may see a fake smile, visible in the teeth but not in the eyes, a shifty gaze which doesn't quite meet yours. You may feel a limp hand-shake, hear a voice that says 'yes' and a body that says 'no'. Their manner may be over-confident, insecure or slippery; they may quickly change their mind to say what they think you want to hear; or they may offer praise or compliments in a tone that lacks emotion or conviction.

As you think of people whose authenticity doesn't quite ring true you may also recognise those who present an overly-polished front, which may be highly professional and controlled and yet reveals nothing of the personality underneath.

These characteristics in isolation may not come from a disingenuous place. We may all have displayed them at some point in our lives because of shyness, insecurity or lack of rapport. However, what we should bear in mind is that when we behave in this way we can appear inauthentic, which in turn can detract from our gravitas.

Having considered what authentic communication is not, let's examine what it *is*. If you think of the most compelling talks you've witnessed it's likely that you remember the person, rather than their sentences, their stories, rather than the facts. A memorable example of authentic communication was Barack Obama's response to the

Newtown School shootings which devastated a Connecticut community. His words, and the genuine emotion that he displayed, were heart-felt, timely and empathic. Authentic because, whether you believe in his politics or not, it was clear that he was experiencing his audience's pain. In allowing his grief and shock to be visible he revealed the true power of authenticity, which is to share in both the strength and vulnerability of humanity.

So what was it about Obama's speech that communicated authenticity? What did he do and say that made this speech genuine and heartfelt? The following extract and subsequent analysis will provide some pointers as you develop your own authentic communication style.

> *'Here, in Newtown, I come to offer the love and prayers of a nation. I am very mindful that mere words cannot match the depths of your sorrow, nor can they heal your wounded hearts.*
>
> *I can only hope it helps for you to know that you're not alone in your grief, that our world, too, has been torn apart, that all across this land of ours, we have wept with you. We've pulled our children tight.*
>
> *And you must know that whatever measure of comfort we can provide, we will provide. Whatever portion of sadness that we can share with you to ease this heavy load, we will gladly bear it. Newtown, you are not alone.'*[12]

Respect for the audience was conveyed through reference to their circumstances, a willingness to see the world from their perspective, with an emphasis on 'you', 'us' and 'we', rather than 'I' and 'me'. Where opinions and beliefs were personal they were 'owned'

---

[12] http://www.guardian.co.uk/world/2012/dec/17/obama-speech-newtown-school-shooting.

through the use of 'I believe', 'I think', 'I hope'. Thoughts were expressed honestly and transparently, emotions expressed with control and dignity. The language was simple, without pomp, jargon, artifice or unnecessary detail. Commitments and promises were made with passion and conviction.

As well as what was said, Obama's non-verbal communication (or body language) also communicated sympathy and support. Gestures were fluid and complemented the words; his eyes connected with the audience through a still and steady gaze, even though he would occasionally look down at his notes. The body was at ease, the stance relaxed, open and unguarded. The voice flowed freely, with emotions expressed through pitch and tone.

As you develop your own authentic communication style, take some time to observe how leaders you admire express their authenticity and gravitas. For advice on how to model leaders, turn to the final chapter of this book.

Developing an authentic communication style

As you encourage your authentic self to emerge you may find that you want to express yourself in a more natural style too.

Your state of mind will directly influence how you come across. If you are feeling flustered, uncomfortable or distracted, you will be less likely to convey your best authentic self than if you are feeling calm, confident and well prepared. As Ingrid Bergman said: 'Be yourself. The world worships the original' and you should take time to remind yourself of the unique qualities that got you to where you are today.

Create a series of statements that reinforce your right to be yourself, a pep-talk that celebrates the authentic you. One client concocted this fabulous mantra, which she repeats whenever she is going into a challenging situation: 'I have a right to be in this room, in this meeting, on this podium. I have an interesting and relevant point of view to share based on my unique experience of life. Just as I am fascinated by other peoples' views, so they will be drawn to my opinions, because they are based on my unshakable principles and ideals.'

Although revealing the 'real you' is important, it's equally important to ensure your ego doesn't take over entirely! Find opportunities to reveal your emotions and imperfections, while selecting those that will contribute to your authenticity and gravitas rather than damaging your credibility. Another useful technique is to focus on the other person, with your intention being 'what can I learn from you?' rather than 'what can I tell you?'; 'how can I help you?' rather than 'what can you do for me?'

The words you choose will also go a long way to illustrate authenticity. When introducing yourself, find ways to draw together the professional and the personal 'you' through the stories your share. Anecdotes are like gifts, which when bestowed will make you memorable and create a connection, particularly if you relate them to the other person's experiences.

As you think about what you're going to say, speak from the heart as well as the head. Be rational, yes, but back up your facts with gut instinct and passion. Consider also how you can harness your emotions to suit your purpose. Emotion unbridled can be alarming and even off-putting. Emotion that conveys the right tone will live long after you've stopped speaking. If you want your audience to feel concerned about a situation, show that concern yourself, but link it to a rational solution. If you feel passionate about a topic, show that passion yourself, but help them to understand the reasons why.

Rather than the passive 'it is thought' or 'some people say', consider 'I believe' to relay conviction, while taking care through your tone to avoid sounding pompous or preachy. You could also try the disarmingly honest 'I think' or 'from my experience', as long as what you say has some substance behind it.

You can also consider humour to counterbalance the strength of your message and 'keep it real'. This shouldn't be about cracking rude jokes, being the class clown, laughing at a colleague or being overly self-deprecating. Humour should always be delivered from a generous heart and appropriate to the prevailing culture. Although a short-hand expression of authentic feelings, swearing can be offensive to some people, so go with what feels right to you, while respecting the sensibilities of the people you're with.

While wanting to be open, beware of giving so much away that you lose your authority, an integral part of gravitas. An authentic leader is different from an honest fool, who wants to be everyone's friend, or negates their position by making excuses like 'I'm not very good at this', 'I haven't prepared enough' or 'I'm not sure I made sense there'. It's as much about what you don't say as what you say. No one has the time or inclination to listen to a lengthy diatribe or a convoluted shaggy dog story. Pick stories that are relevant and learn when it's time to hold your tongue to maintain your mystique.

Your non-verbal communication will contribute just as much to your authenticity as the words you choose. Look people in the eye, hold their gaze for a couple of seconds and respond to what you see there. Some people are happy to hold eye contact, others will find it an intrusion. The fact that you initiate this level of contact will not only make you appear confident, but also help you to feel more confident too. Your eyes are the window to your soul and there is something liberating about letting people see what's behind them.

Your body can also help you to express authenticity. An open posture, with arms wide, chest open and feet pointing subtly outwards projects a sense of pride and that you have nothing to hide. Conversely, a closed posture can indicates a lack of confidence and even a need for self-protection, as though you had something to hide.

Staying authentic through challenging times

Staying true to our authentic selves is most critical when we find ourselves under pressure – whether delivering a tough message, selling a product we're not sure about, presenting to a hostile audience, or networking in a room full of strangers.

The temptation here is to bring in jargon, hide behind facts and figures, talk too much or too little. Our physical presence is compromised; our body language, voice and facial expressions appear forced or stilted.

People with authenticity often display a level of vulnerability, a quality that Brené Brown referred to as a 'secret ingredient to influence' during a TED Talk that she gave in 2010.[13] Brown is a research professor at the University of Houston and has spent the past ten years studying human behaviour and authenticity.

In her talk she spoke about how vulnerability enables us to connect with others on a deeper level than we might be used to, influencing authentically through who we are rather than what we do.

If you watch leaders with authenticity, you will notice that, particularly in challenging times, they are prepared to show their vulnerability, carefully balancing their strengths with weaknesses that will not detract from their overall impact. This is not about bursting into tears at the first sign of a struggle. This is about being prepared to show your humanity, to share your emotions at appropriate moments, and demonstrate honesty and integrity in a challenging world.

---

[13] TED (Technology, Entertainment and Design) is a global set of conferences owned by the private non-profit Sapling Foundation, formed to disseminate "ideas worth spreading". In November 2012 TED Talks had been watched one billion times worldwide, reflecting a still growing global audience. Brené Brown has spoken for TED twice, once in 2010 and again in 2012.

When you know that you're about to go into a challenging situation remember the following tips:

Five tips for challenging situations

1. Begin by reminding yourself of your purpose, role, identity, values, beliefs – what makes you authentically you – and your right to be in the room.

2. Focus on the present – not what's gone before or what's going to happen – the here and now.

3. Take the time to breathe, notice the air coming into your lungs, the physical sensation of release as you breathe out and the way that the very act of breathing relaxes your body, frees your mind and loosens up your posture.

4. Spend a few moments connecting with the people in the room; remind yourself of the reason you're there and the rapport you've already created.

5. Feel the earth beneath your feet, take strength from its solidity and think about how good you will feel when you know that you have been true to yourself and done yourself justice in what you're about to do and say.

Another barrier to authenticity might be shyness or a lack of confidence, where a workplace persona might feel like a useful shield, a safer option than exposing too much of your inner being. However, in a world which expects some degree of performance, whatever role you're playing, keeping up the shield may prevent you from making authentic connections and realising your full potential.

Little by little, find ways to be bold and let your authentic self be seen. Be the first with your views in a brainstorm, find ways to incorporate a personal story into your presentations, challenge yourself to reveal something of your private self to five people at a networking event. In time, you will become more accustomed to revealing your authentic self, which will increase your confidence and help you to lead with gravitas.

If you appreciate the benefits of authenticity at work and want to get there, you will, not by trying too hard, but by letting go. Trying to be *more* authentic is like looking for a pot of gold at the end of a rainbow: the more you think about being authentic, the more self-conscious you get and the less authentic you become. Authenticity resides in the full spectrum of colour held within the rainbow.

Knowing how to channel your authentic self is an invaluable life skill. In time, you will instinctively know how to harness your best self to achieve your aims as a leader. You will be able to detect people who are authentic and genuine, and those pretending to be someone else, consciously or subconsciously.

In appreciating the challenges of finding your own authentic self you will have compassion for those who are struggling to forge their unique identity, and reach out to them to create a bond which will encourage them to let themselves be seen. When you allow your authentic colours to emerge naturally, then your gravitas will truly shine.

Chapter 4

Presence

'And, as we let our own light shine, we consciously give other people permission to do the same. As we are liberated from our fear, our presence automatically liberates others.'

• Marianne Williamson •

Presence is the fourth segment of the Gravitas Wheel©; the first external component that can be perceived by others; an outward expression of who you are. Presence is an intangible quality. You

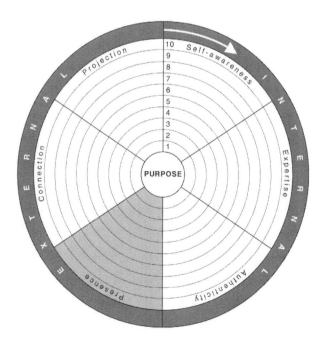

know when someone has it, even though you may not be able to put your finger on exactly what it is. Whether it's an actor on stage, a face across a crowded room or the only person in a meeting who seems to hold everyone's attention, it's a quality that captivates and intrigues. And because people naturally gravitate towards those they find intriguing, it's a valuable quality to possess if you're looking to build gravitas.

For today's leaders, the ability to capture and hold attention is crucial. Without presence, people may not notice you as you enter a room. They may not remember your name, or which department you belong to. You may not be selected for promotion, even though you are more than qualified for the role. You may find it difficult being heard in meetings and get interrupted regularly. You may find yourself ignored at networking events, or struggle to engage your teams.

Although it may sometimes feel easier to keep a low profile, actively cultivating a presence – and knowing how and when to 'dial it up' when you need to – is key to building your gravitas and getting the recognition you deserve at work. Central to any leader's role is the ability to engage, persuade, motivate and inspire. You want your clients, customers, shareholders, board members and colleagues to listen to and respect you in negotiations, debates, conflicts and speeches, whether delivering good, bad or indifferent news. You want your teams to be inspired to follow you, care enough to give you their full attention, and do their utmost to deliver their very best.

Presence is an attractive and compelling leadership quality. Unlike charisma, which can be whimsical, ego-led and skin-deep, leaders with presence radiate strength, sincerity and a sense of substance below the surface.

If you are looking to build gravitas, it is presence combined with the other elements of the Gravitas Wheel© which will give you lasting impact and influence. *Self-awareness* will bring purpose and direction, *Expertise* will give you substance, *Authenticity* will keep you grounded and *Connection* will draw you closer to others. For times when you want to leave an even stronger impression or reach larger audiences, *Projection* will enable you to amplify your message even further.

What is presence?

Dictionary definitions for 'presence' refer to the state of 'being present', the 'personal bearing of a person, especially of a dignified nature', an 'immediate proximity' or 'invisible spirit felt to be nearby'. Stage presence is described as 'the ability to command an audience with impressive style or manner'.

When it comes to leading with gravitas, presence is a combination of all the above. People with presence command attention like a magnet just by being in the room. They possess an aura which holds an audience spell-bound. They radiate an energy that inspires and attracts others. People sit up, take notice and follow their lead.

Presence is a quality possessed by many stars of the stage and screen. Think of Marlene Dietrich, Fred Astaire, Grace Kelly, Marilyn Monroe, Elvis Presley and, more recently, Freddie Mercury, Helen Mirren and Ben Kingsley. Stars of the silver screen and silent movies have been frequently described as having presence, indicating that even when layers of sensory detail like colour and sound have been stripped away, the essence of presence still remains.[14]

Presence is also a characteristic of history's most iconic leaders: think of Martin Luther King's 'I have a dream' address; the first speech that Nelson Mandela gave in 1990 after his release from prison; Aung San Suu Kyi's peaceful protest against the dictatorship of U Ne Win; or, more recently, Malala Yousafzai's speech to the

---

[14] For an example of presence in action, watch Jean Dujardin in *The Artist*, a film about the demise of silent movies.

United Nations in defiance of the Taliban. These examples indicate that presence is not only how a person comes across physically, but also the intensity of their message.

How does presence come across?

Presence is a characteristic of some of the most respected business and community leaders, TV and radio presenters, journalists and newsreaders, who combine the enigmatic quality of movie stars with the significance and weight of political leaders.

We also come across people with presence every day. Recent examples I've observed include an Italian CEO rallying the troops in a company meeting. A man with boundless energy who strode into the room, immediately took charge of the conversation and at one point vaulted over a desk to get to the centre of the room so he could see everyone. Through his speech, I saw a leader with passion and authenticity, someone who would go to the ends of the earth to defend his company, a leader who was not only emotionally but physically capable of leading a battle charge. As well as his physical presence, I saw a leader with an ability to make everyone in the room feel special, expressing his appreciation through shared experiences, citing people by name and engaging them in his stories.

Another example of presence in action is the TED Talk by Benjamin Zander[15], a conductor of the Boston Philharmonic, who began his talk with a story about shoes, parodied himself by striking cartoonish poses, waving his arms around and widening his eyes so far that even the person at the back of the auditorium could see the expression there. In his allocated 18 minutes, he took his audience

---

[15] Benjamin Zander's TED Talk: The transformative power of classical music. February 2008.

on such a powerful journey that by the end the whole audience was physically moved by his message, even though the topic, classical music, was one that, by his own admission, only a small percentage would be engaged by.

Although these people are all very different examples of presence, they do have a number of traits in common, traits which you can develop yourself as you build your own presence and gravitas:

- Passion: a positive energy and commitment to a cause, message or purpose.
- Inner strength: an ability to draw energy and confidence from within rather than relying on others for validation and approval.
- Individuality: a sense of being at ease in one's own skin; being comfortable standing out from the crowd.
- Attraction: a magnetic quality that draws attention either through physical appearance, a compelling voice, a powerful message or a combination of all three.
- Likeability: a quality that inspires admiration and trust and inspires people to follow your lead.
- Mystique: the impression that something is being held back, either through a desire for privacy or to conserve energy.

People with presence also share characteristics that you can see, hear and feel, which help them to stand out from the crowd. Neuroscientific research indicates that in a world full of stimulation and distraction our brains notice what's unusual and remember what's different. It's the same with presence. People with presence stand out because they are different. We remember them because they don't blend into the surroundings.

How does presence come across?

Non-verbal communication	Lack of Presence	Presence
Mindset	Distracted, stressed, nervous, tired	Uncluttered, calm, focused
Body	In pain, hampered, sluggish	At ease, comfortable, energised
Posture	Closed, tense, twisted, asymmetrical	Open, relaxed, aligned, symmetrical
Voice	Shrill, monotone, flat	Steady, melodic, resonant
Eyes	Darting, glazed, dull	Clear, direct, unwavering
Image	Bland, conformist, over-done	Individual, stylish, colourful

Let's explore how this 'difference' comes across in what you see, hear and feel. As we do so, consider the qualities you already display that contribute to your presence and what you can do to develop your presence further.

What you see

We live in a snap judgement world. The impression we make of people is dictated, in a few seconds, predominantly by what we see. If you think of an actor or a ballet dancer, a model or a sportsman, there will be something about how they hold themselves and their physicality which will 'arrest' your attention. If you look at a group of uniformed school children, there will be some that will catch your eye and others that won't.

Visual cues include an open and relaxed posture, as opposed to one that is closed and tense. Think of Mo Farah or Serena Williams: fluid rather than jerking movements, a body that's both at ease and ready for action, comfortable and energised, as opposed to hampered, sluggish or in pain. When someone with presence is talking, their face will be relaxed and animated, lit up from the inside; their eyes will hold you in a steady gaze rather than darting around.

People with presence often have a style that stands out: they may have a signature colour, item of jewellery or piece of clothing that 'is them'. They are unlikely to be bland or conformist on the one hand, or over-made up or stylised on the other.

What you hear

A person's presence will be eloquently conveyed through their voice and breathing patterns. If you listen to sports commentary on the radio, whether it's the buzz and burble of the cricket pitch, the intense hum of the race track or the highs and lows of the football field, your attention will be captivated through the energy in the commentator's voice. Presence comes across through a vocal range which traverses pitch, volume and cadence, a rich and unexpected vocabulary or an unusual accent. Presence can also be enhanced through breathing patterns, with free, deep and steady breathing exuding calmness, solidity and ease, as opposed to the discomfort associated with irregular, shallow or hampered breath.

What you feel

Emotional state is also directly linked to presence. If an individual's demeanour is focused, confident and energised, they will have more presence than if they are distracted, tired or stressed out. The emotion that a person evokes in others will also increase or decrease their presence. If you meet someone who is inspiring and engaging, or if they express a strong emotion freely, you will remember their presence far longer than if they are bored, disinterested or have an apathetic attitude or watered-down communication style.

Developing your own presence

While it may seem like some people have 'it' and others don't, we were all born with a natural presence. If you observe a child playing, you will see it in the intensity of their gaze, hear it in their laughter and sense it in their ability to be entirely absorbed in the present moment.

Although the purity of a child's presence may diminish over time, as adults we still have the quality within us, and can learn to bring it to the fore if we choose to. Presence occurs when a person is highly attuned to their surroundings; very much 'in the room' as opposed to being wrapped up in their own thoughts. You can think of presence as a *passive* or *active* state. Passive presence is a glow or aura that hangs in the air around a person even when they're doing nothing: think of the one person you notice in a crowded train carriage or the only delegate you remember at a busy conference. Active presence is the energy that emanates when a person 'switches on' to perform: think of an enigmatic speaker or, at its extreme, the energy of the pop star who can make the person at the back of the auditorium think they are singing directly to them.

If you would like to develop your presence, it can be helpful to think of it as a flame, whose intensity you can increase or decrease depending on the impact you'd like to make. At its core, presence is paying attention to the present moment and, in doing so, creating an energy which you can then radiate outwards. The more energy you generate from within, the more you radiate outwards.

As a leader you will be faced with various circumstances which will require different levels of presence. There may be times when you want to keep a low profile, perhaps entering or exiting a meeting unnoticed. In these situations you will hide your light under a bushel, keep your head down, avoid eye contact, direct your attention inwards. There will be other occasions when you want to be noticed, but not the centre of attention – perhaps in a meeting where you want everyone to get the air time they deserve. In these circumstances, your presence will come across as a subtle glow which says 'I'm here' but doesn't overpower.

You will also experience situations when you want to leave a strong and lasting impression – perhaps to draw attention to your company's accomplishments in a competitive pitch or impress a panel in a job interview. In these situations, you will want to let your qualities and experience shine and so your presence will appear as a strong flame, burning brightly. In large group situations, for example company meetings or networking events, you will want to radiate a presence that touches everyone, even though you may not be able to connect with them all personally. In those instances, you will increase the intensity of your flame, exuding a smouldering warmth that reaches a roomful and makes everyone feel like they have spoken to you personally.

In situations when you want to make a powerful impact, perhaps delivering a keynote or town hall speech to an auditorium, you will want to project a shining beacon of light which attracts the attention of everyone there. In those situations, you will need the skills of projection, which are explored in the *Projection* chapter.

Presence zappers

As well as understanding the different levels of presence, and which will be appropriate in various circumstances, it is also helpful to be aware of presence zappers, and how to overcome them. We have all experienced the difference between being present – connected to the here and now – and absent, lost in our own thoughts or distracted from what's going on around us. In a high pressure work environment it's very easy to become caught up by conflicting priorities, juggling an increasing list of tasks with an ever decreasing amount of time, rushing towards the next deadline, chasing the next promotion, without having the chance to take a step back and reflect.

An obsession with speed is the quickest way to lose presence. In a busy work environment, we can find ourselves moving so fast that we become disconnected from ourselves, let alone the world around us. In flying from appointment to appointment or project to project, we limit possibilities for human connection and make only a fleeting impression on others.

Nerves, which often show up as voices inside our heads telling us that we're not good enough, experienced enough or practiced enough to do whatever we're about to do, also have a huge impact on our ability to be present and have presence. Sometimes these voices can distort reality, becoming so insistent that it's difficult to pay attention to our real surroundings.

In addition to real-life and self-perpetuated distractions, our attention is increasingly drawn by technology: the ultimate presence zapper. We would rather use email or instant messenger than pick up the phone. It's much quicker to send out a PowerPoint deck than explain our point of view in real time. We check our phone for emails, texts, social media and the internet from the moment we wake up to the moment we go to bed, with research showing the average person checks their phone 110 times a day and up to every six seconds in the evenings.[16] When we look at our phone we are looking downwards rather than outwards, directing our gaze to an inanimate object rather than to the people around us. We are sending out a message which says the virtual world encapsulated in our hands is more interesting than the real world around us. With such a powerful attention-grabber welded to our side 24/7, it's no wonder that our presence is being zapped.

Switching on to your presence

If you're looking to increase your presence, the first step is deciding to put your attention 100 percent on the present moment. In focusing on what's going on around you, rather than what's going on in your head or on your phone, you will automatically stand out from the crowd and create an attractive energy which will draw people towards you.

---

[16] http://www.dailymail.co.uk/sciencetech/article-2449632/How-check-phone-The-average-person-does-110-times-DAY-6-seconds-evening.html.

You can then use a series of techniques to increase your presence. Planning ahead will help you to feel in control, although rather than purely thinking about what you're going to say, you can use OPRAHS, a memorable acronym which has been designed to help you to plan more effectively.

Objective	What are you and the other people there to achieve?
Purpose	What's your personal reason for being there?
Role	What role will you choose to adopt to suit the circumstances? For example, facilitator, chair, strategist, tactician
Attitude	What attitude will it be most helpful for you to adopt, given the above? For example, excited, curious, concerned, playful or challenging
Hear	Rather than focusing solely on what you're going to say, pay attention instead to how you're going to listen to other people's points of view.
Say	You will now be in a strong position to consider how you can make the most valuable contribution to the meeting. Having thought this through in advance, you will be more able to influence the direction of the discussion and more likely to present yourself with gravitas rather than worrying about what you're going to say and when.

As you go into the situation, make a decision that you are going to 'switch on', bringing as much energy and attention to the present moment as you can. Key to this is eliminating distractions. Remove all technological devices from sight or earshot, having decided when you will next check in to stop your mind from wandering. If an urgent or important thought creeps into your mind, make a note of it, and then bring your attention back to the present.

Looking to your surroundings will also help keep you present and distract you from any negative thoughts. Carefully observe the people around you – their expressions, their gestures, their points of view – *choose* to be fascinated by what they say rather than disengage. Connect with people using a mixture of your senses: look them in the eye, ask questions that demonstrate your interest in them, listen and reflect back their responses. Think of communication as an exchange of gifts and consider what you can bring that will make a positive and memorable impression. Notice the energy and warmth that's created when you decide to connect with other people and how, by paying attention to them, they are more likely to pay it back to you through their attention and focus.

With the best will in the world, staying present to our surroundings can be tiring. If you do find your mind drifting off, gently bring your thoughts back to the present, tune into what you can see and hear around you, the temperature in the room, the points people are making and how they are interacting with one another. After a few moments of just noticing what's going on, turn your mind to how you can contribute

As you become more adept at being present, you will find yourself more able to develop connections with the people in the room, react spontaneously to what's going on and make more of a lasting impression on the group. That way, you will begin to feel more present and other people will begin to notice your presence too.

Jessica

The challenge of remaining present was experienced by Jessica, a senior director in a software manufacturing company, who had been advised to increase her executive presence in the run up to a merger. A self-proclaimed introvert, she was extremely good at deflecting attention away from herself and keeping a low profile. On the one hand, she loved her 'invisibility cloak' and could slip silently in and out of meetings without being noticed. On the other hand, she hated being ignored and knew that, in order to progress she would need to find a way to raise her profile.

Through coaching, Jessica realised that 95 percent of the time she was wrapped up in thoughts which she didn't want interrupted by other people. As such, she preferred working alone and hated the attention she received when leading teams.

The first step towards creating presence came when Jessica agreed that for a certain period of time she would concentrate on 'being present' with the people in the room, and monitor the response she received. She chose team meetings as a starting point and decided not only to focus on the topics under discussion, but also the people in the room: their ideas, their communication style and mannerisms. In time she realised that she could increase and decrease the amount of energy she radiated outwards through the amount of attention she placed on the people and the present moment. The more energy and interest she directed at people the more energy and warmth she would receive back. Although she found being this 'present' tiring and acknowledged that she would never radiate the same level of presence that a more extrovert colleague might, she appreciated the increased rapport she experienced with her colleagues and found that her profile increased as a result.

....
Exercise
....

Identify three opportunities over the next month when you would like to 'be present' – compare sitting on a train on your journey to work (when being present isn't necessary and in fact any distraction is welcome!) and making an impact in your company meeting.

Apply the 'switching on' techniques to each situation and reflect on the impact that being present has on your appreciation of the world around you and on your gravitas.

Increasing your presence in different situations

As well as knowing how to become more present to the world around you, you can also 'dial up' your presence to increase your impact in different situations. Radiating presence is all about directing energy outwards in such a way that it draws attention to you so you stand out from the crowd.

Start by finding out how your 'presence' comes across to others when you're on top form. This will give you clues as to what you can do to increase your presence at will. Ask one or two trusted colleagues to provide feedback on your presence in various settings, for example delivering a talk, participating in a meeting and talking with your team. Ask them to share what they saw, heard and felt comparing when you had presence with when you didn't. Think also about people you admire with presence, what they do to amplify their impact and what you can emulate.

Now that you have a greater understanding of your own presence, you can learn how to access it at will and amplify it when needed. The following techniques will enable you to experience different levels of presence and dial them up or down to suit different situations.

Set the dial

Reflect on the times when you'd like to make an impact. Identify whether you'd like your 'flame' to be perceived as a subtle glow, or whether you'd like to increase its intensity to become a shining light. As you think about the situation you're going into, decide where on the dial you want your presence to be. Is it a keynote speech or a 'meet and greet'? Are you chairing a meeting or attending it? What do you want people to know and remember about you after you've left the room? What is your message, to what extent do you believe it and how will you communicate it with conviction? All this will help you to decide whether you want a subtle glow, a strong flame, a bright light or a shining beacon.

Create a positive mindset

Having a mantra or affirmation that you can utter out loud or in your head is a great technique for radiating confidence and presence as well as minimising nerves. Dorothy Sarnoff was a Broadway actress and voice coach who developed a copyrighted formula for 'owning the room', which you can recite to yourself when you would like your presence to be felt. It consists of four statements:

- 'I'm glad *I'm* here': this helps you to approach any situation with a smile on your face and anticipating the best outcome.
- 'I'm glad *you're* here': this takes attention away from how you're feeling to what is going on for your audience and the people around you.
- 'I *care* about you': this shows your appreciation for your audience and encourages warmth back from them.
- 'I *know* that I know': this encourages you to trust your expertise, connect with your authenticity and instinct and be secure in the knowledge that, whatever happens, you will make the right choices in what you choose to say and do.

Using your breath and body

Managing your breathing will also help you to stay present and control nerves. Breathe air deeply into your diaphragm, filling your lungs with oxygen and holding it for a few seconds before breathing out. This will give you energy, bring a sense of openness and vitality and prevent your attention from drifting.

The way you position your body is also directly linked to your ability to radiate a strong and confident presence. Research conducted by Amy Cuddy, a social psychologist and researcher at Harvard University, found that by adopting strong and powerful postures – think Wonder Woman or Superman on a good day – for just two minutes, has a fundamental effect on your confidence levels.[17]

Start by planting your feet on the ground, placing them directly underneath your hips and shoulders, with your weight evenly distributed. Feel the solidity of the ground beneath you, the gravity of the earth drawing you down. Now imagine that you have a string running all the way through the middle of your body and out through the top of your head. Take hold of the string and pull it up gently. Notice how this aligns each vertebrae along your spine, making you stand taller and grow in stature. Bring your shoulders back and down, draw your belly in and tuck your bottom under. If you're in a chair, sit *up*, positioning your backside squarely in your chair and leaning forward slightly. This will keep you energised, 'in the room' and attract attention to you.

If you're walking into a room, walk with purpose and intent. Before you cross the threshold, put your shoulders down and back, open up your chest, look up at the ceiling for a short moment, smile, and then stride into the room, imagining the air parting before you as you enter.

You can also modulate your body language to communicate different messages and convey either approachability or credibility.

---

[17] Check out Amy Cuddy's TED Talk: Your body language shapes who you are. June 2012

Michael Grinder, non-verbal communication expert, refers to these styles as 'approachable dog' and 'credible cat'[18]. The approachable dog style is useful when you want to build rapport, open up a conversation, elicit people's views or lighten a mood. You will choose open, expansive gestures with palms turned up; your posture will be asymmetrical with plenty of movement; there will be lots of eye contact and smiles and you will have a friendly tone with a voice that goes up at the end of sentences. The credible cat style is appropriate when you'd like to assert your views, relay serious information, share opinions without being interrupted, shut down conversations and bring the meeting to a close. You will have a symmetrical posture; your movements and gestures will be minimal; you will keep your palms down rather than up; you will adopt a serious tone with plenty of pauses and your voice will go down at the end of your sentences.

Turning up the dial

If you are not getting the attention you need, or if you want to make an even more powerful and lasting impression, you can amplify your presence by adopting the following techniques:

- Be the first: Find opportunities to speak first, volunteer first or answer a question first. Going first conveys confidence, draws attention and asserts your presence but shouldn't be overplayed as it can be perceived as arrogance and prevents others' views from being heard.

- Look different: Choose clothes that attract attention. Compare the woman in the red dress to the one in the hoody and jeans; the man in the Saville Row suit, sharp tie and cufflinks to the one in the chinos and polo shirt; the suit in a roomful of jeans or the jeans in a roomful of suits.

---

[18] Charisma, the Art of Relationships. Michael Grinder. November 2010.

- Be maverick: There are times when a slight quirkiness can create presence more memorably than anything else. Consider what you can do or say that may be considered slightly shocking or off-beam, whilst taking care to respect the culture and people you're with.

- Dramatise: Decide to draw people to you by making your space an attractive and fun place to be. Emulate the energy of the person who holds court at the most exciting parties: stand up straighter, walk taller, speak louder than you usually might. Exaggerate your gestures and enhance your facial expressions in the same way as you would to attract the attention of a waiter in a busy restaurant, or a barman in a busy pub.

- Highlight: If your voice isn't being heard, make an unexpected movement that 'cuts into' the room, clear your throat, laugh or use attention-grabbing openers like 'The best thing about this is…', 'The most exciting news is that…', 'The most important thing to consider here…'. This isn't about becoming a caricature of yourself, but more an affirmation of who you are, asserting your right to be in the room.

As we prepare to move onto the *Connection* chapter, I'd like to leave you with this final thought. In learning how to be present, you will not only increase your impact, but also give yourself the time and space to appreciate the world around you. In adding presence to other elements of the Gravitas Wheel© – *Expertise, Authenticity, Self-awareness* and *Connection* – you will be combining the qualities of the most enigmatic actor with the power of the most compelling script, giving you the confidence and gravitas to fulfil your role as leader and attract the attention you and your message deserve.

Chapter 5

Connection

*'The most interesting space is
where I end and you begin.'*

• David Hockney •

Connection is the fifth segment of the Gravitas Wheel© and the one
that most directly reveals your gravitas to the people around you.
In today's business environment your ability to connect is crucial.
You can have all the *Self-awareness, Expertise, Authenticity, Presence*
and *Projection* in the world, but unless you can share those qualities
with others you will severely compromise your impact.

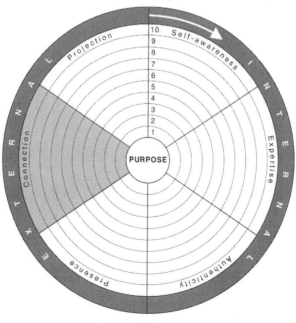

Many organisations are moving from a traditional hierarchical model to a matrix structure. Many teams are now made up of subject matter experts with no designated 'line of command'. In this environment, the ability to influence without authority is critical to delivering results and progressing in your career.

In an overly-marketed and packaged-up world, we have become cynical of people who approach us with the sole intention of selling us something or getting something from us. We are sceptical of leaders who say all the right things about vision, mission and engagement, but don't take the time to listen to what we think or reveal anything about themselves. We see straight through salespeople who look us in the eye, give us a firm handshake and use our name three times in the first sentence.

What we are looking for is people who understand us and genuinely have our best interests at heart: leaders with a gravitas that we aspire to who can also create authentic connections with the people around them.

Creating connections is a key skill for leading with gravitas in today's business world. While leaders with traditional gravitas are respected, they can sometimes be perceived as aloof and distant, lacking the warmth and sparkle of their more charismatic colleagues. Although this aloofness may have been admired in the past, it is not a quality which will endear you in today's workplace. As you develop gravitas, your ability to connect is what will keep you down to earth and accessible. Having connected, people will *want* to deliver results for you, not because you're their boss, but because they like and respect you. Having built rapport with them, you will know instinctively how to motivate and inspire them and how to adapt your style to suit their needs.

As well as enhancing your leadership capability in your immediate workplace, connection will also help you to maximise your reach on a wider scale, whether you are part of an organisation or run your own company. In a large corporate environment, and particularly in a global setting, it may not always be possible to have direct contact with people whose opinions may have a bearing on your success. This makes it even more important to build a broad network of people whose influence extends beyond your personal reach, who know you well enough to recommend you and make introductions when the time comes.

The perception of gravitas comes not only through the impression you make, but also your reputation which is based on what people know about you and what they say about you when you're not there. Although this isn't fully within your control, what is, is the amount of effort you put into building connections and the impression you make during those interactions.

In addition to the professional benefits of connecting, the personal benefits should not be underestimated. The higher up you go in an organisation, the less likely you will receive support from a line manager or team leader. Likewise, being your own boss can be a lonely place as you juggle the multiple responsibilities of bringing in the business and delivering for your customers. Research has shown that human connection is more closely linked to happiness than wealth, fame and even physical health, and that the positive feelings we get from co-operating with others activate the 'reward' areas of the brain in a similar way as the satisfaction of hunger. Conversely, it has been shown that when we experience social rejection, we feel it in the same areas of the brain as physical pain[19].

In an increasingly virtual world, where much of the contact we have is via email, text, SMS or social networking, the ability to make meaningful – and real – connections is more important than ever

---

[19] http://www.psychologytoday.com/blog/connections/200905/epidemic-loneliness.

before. Social and professional networking sites make it easy to connect with a large volume of people at the touch of a button, which might make you feel popular and important. However if you spend all your time amassing contacts, how much time will you have left over to build quality relationships with people who will appreciate your gravitas in real time?

Although human connection may appear to be the most natural skill in the world, the danger is that if you spend your whole time communicating via your PC, laptop or phone, you may get out of the habit of making natural connections face to face. Relationships are created through effort on both sides: you *make* conversation and *pay* someone attention, it doesn't just happen. And this learnt ability to connect is like a muscle which, if not exercised regularly, will begin to lose its strength and power. Virtual communication has its place; however, if you replace real time connection with phone or screen time you may miss the subtle nuances in communication that you pick up when you're both in the same room, nuances which unnoticed or ignored can lead to misunderstandings and a breakdown in rapport. Communicating entirely by virtual means will also mean that you limit the emotional rewards that you get from real time connection, which we all need to thrive and feel satisfied at work.

Connection: the secret ingredient to gravitas

The word 'connection' is defined by the Oxford English Dictionary as 'a relationship in which a person or thing is linked or associated with something else'. The definition for 'connections' is 'people with whom one has social or professional contact or to whom one is related, especially those with influence and able to offer one help'.

When it comes to leading with gravitas, both these definitions are relevant. To progress in a competitive environment, you need to build meaningful relationships with others. To accelerate your progression, you need to build a network of people to whom you can turn for support in achieving your goals.

The good news is that, whether you're a natural-born people person or not, your ability to connect will be greatly enhanced when you tap into the qualities represented in the rest of your Gravitas Wheel©. Through building *Self-awareness* you will appreciate which facets of your personality will most appeal to different people and when. Through choosing to share your *Authentic* self you will make genuine connections with people who appreciate the real you. Through sharing your *Expertise* you will pique people's interest and create the potential for common ground. In revealing your *Presence* and choosing to 'be present' you will naturally draw others to you. And in knowing how to *Project* you will find ways to attract attention when you need to connect from afar.

Sarah Matthew is co-owner of a healthcare communications agency and a self-confessed 'connector'. Her passion for people is born out of genuine curiosity about what makes them tick and a generous open-hearted intention to help them succeed. Sarah shares the belief of many successful leaders that if you find ways to help other people achieve their purpose, opportunities to succeed will come your way too.

Her view is that, for long-lasting success, the key to connection is another segment of the Gravitas Wheel©: authenticity: 'if you build relationships based on authenticity you will create trust. Once trust is created, the business opportunities will follow.'

Dave Clarke

This sentiment is shared by Dave Clarke, CEO of NRG Networking, who describes networking as 'making friends with people and finding ways to help them out'. He believes that the first step to business success is building rapport and that people will be far more likely to choose you, your products and your services if they like and respect you.

In a busy work environment it may sometimes be tempting to sacrifice time getting to know people for time delivering deadlines. Whereas previously meetings would take place in a room, around a table, with people arriving early or staying late for a chat, they are now more likely to be held via back-to-back conference calls, with little time to get to know each another in between, let alone create a perception of gravitas.

Margot James

Margot James, MP, former Vice Chair of the Conservative Party and previously CEO of a successful PR company, observes that, whether in parliament or in the boardroom, it is often those off-duty moments before and after meetings when the most useful information is shared and longstanding working relationships built. She advises, 'To build a profile for yourself you need to build positive relationships. Although the temptation with a busy workload might be to dash in and out, people with the strongest influence tend to arrive early and build time into their diaries to stay for a chat after the meeting, both about the work at hand and, in time, on a more social level. In politics, as in business, it's just as much about who you know as what you know'.

When it comes to gravitas, it is the people who appear to have time for others who make the greatest connections and impact. Consider those who rush in just as a meeting is about to start, speak quickly, interrupt others, drum their fingers on the desk, check their Blackberry twenty times and then rush out again. Contrast with people who arrive early, speak at a measured pace, take the time to draw in and listen to each participant's view, and then depart calmly, once they have said goodbye to everyone in the room.

And so, with all this in mind, how can you maximise the precious time you have to cultivate connections that will enhance your gravitas now and in years to come?

The ability to make meaningful connections is based on firstly, creating a diverse and mutually supportive network and secondly, having the personal skills to build rapport. We will now look at the practical steps you can take to achieve this.

Planning your networking strategy

With the best will in the world, you can't connect with everyone. From a professional perspective, the people most likely to reach their goals are those who have a clear purpose in mind and actively connect with those who can relate to that purpose in some way. Where there is common ground there will also be the potential for practical and moral support, and the opportunity for both parties to help each other to achieve their goals.

In order to build gravitas, and make the most of the time you have for forging connections, the first step is to remind yourself of your overall purpose in life, and what you're in business *for* or, as Stephen Covey put it in *The Seven Habits of Highly Effective People*: 'Start with the end in mind'. You can do this by connecting with yourself at the levels of purpose, identity, values and beliefs by completing

• 99 •

the Logical Levels of Change pyramid and revisiting your goals in the *Self-awareness* chapter.

Once you're clear on your purpose and goals, the next step is to build a mutually-supportive network. A useful metaphor for planning your networking strategy is a map, with *global* connections being the world-class leaders in your field, *national* connections being those who are currently beyond your immediate reach, and *local* connections being people currently in your network. Although the easiest tactic might be to make connections at a local level, the most effective route to success is to extend your reach to people currently on your horizon. It is by connecting with the people on the outskirts of your world that you will succeed in making your current world bigger, thereby increasing your influence and fulfilling your true potential.

Exercise

As you plan your networking strategy take some time to consider global, national and local connections. On a *global* scale, who are the people you would like to connect with and why? Think BIG: the world's leading expert, the most successful entrepreneur, the most respected thought-leader in your field. The aim here is to expand your world and open up opportunities for the most enriching connections.

On a *national* scale, who are the people currently outside your immediate circle who could support you in achieving your goals? For example, if you're planning on moving your business into another sector, who are the key influencers and opinion formers who are operating there already? If you're looking to move into another department within your organisation, who are the key decision makers you need to convince?

On a *local* scale, think about the people in your existing network, or those connected to the people in your network, who might relate to your purpose and be inclined to support you. Rather than limiting your thinking to current colleagues, think about all the people you have had positive connections with in the past. Instead of purely focusing on business connections, think about people you know personally who may also relate to your goals and purpose.

As well as thinking about people, consider *organisations* you would like to be associated with, for example networking groups, special interest organisations, professional bodies and social groups. Conduct some research into their remit and membership. If appropriate, decide how you would like to be involved, whether attending events, building contacts or even signing up to their membership.

Once you have identified who you want to connect with you can then create a strategic approach for building relationships with them. Although some of the best connections are created spontaneously, spending a bit of time thinking about the people you would like to meet and how you can support one another can be the difference between a lasting relationship and a missed opportunity.[20]

Building rapport

Having explored how to build a strong and supportive network, let's explore how to make the most of your time with people through developing the skill of rapport.

Rapport is key to building strong connections and is often the reason people choose to work with you rather than anyone else. As a leader, knowing how to build rapport quickly and with diverse people will make it much easier for you to influence teams, clients and other stakeholders.

Although many people believe it's about remembering to talk about someone's dog, children or weekend and matching their body language, rapport goes much deeper than this. It is in fact the ability to connect in a way that creates an environment of shared trust and understanding; an ability to appreciate and accept another's point of view. Rapport can happen instantly: you meet someone and it feels like you've known them forever. It can also grow over time, as you peel away the onion skins of formality and get to know who you both are underneath.

In this section, we are going to explore how you can cultivate rapport with anyone, firstly by creating the most conducive mindset and secondly by adapting your communication style in a way that feels authentic to you.

---

[20] Further advice and a range of downloadable tools are available on the *Leading with Gravitas* website to support you with your networking strategy. Go to www.leadingwithgravitas.com/resources.

Creating a mindset for rapport

The ability to build rapport is founded on having an open attitude combined with a mindset that says you respect and are genuinely interested in the other person, and that you care. The most effective way to do this is by aiming to see the world through their eyes, and then demonstrating that you've heard them and that you value and respect their point of view.

> **Creating a Mindset for Rapport**
> - Openness
> - Honesty
> - Respect
> - Generosity
> - Positivity
> - Ease

Top hairdresser Claire Rendell, who trained with Vidal Sassoon, has built her business around her ability to create rapport. People come to her for a great haircut, but they return year after year because she knows how to make them feel special. As part of her training she was taught how to put people at ease. She was encouraged to keep abreast of current affairs so that she always had interesting subjects to discuss beyond where they had been on their holidays. As well as providing an excellent service, Claire became highly skilled at uncovering people's needs and communicating sensitively. She became adept at reading body language and adapting her approach for every person who came into the salon so that she could manage expectations and give people what they needed. Invaluable skills for a hairdresser; just as critical for business leaders looking to enhance their impact at work.

Claire Rendell

The ability to build rapport with people is particularly important when working with people from different cultures. Mark Connolly, Global CRO at Audience Science, spends the majority of his time working with colleagues and clients from diverse markets and believes that, although it's important to understand different cultures' customs and behaviours, the most important thing is to be sincere, genuine, honest and open. 'In business terms, rapport is built through promising you'll deliver and then exceeding expectations. It is lost through lying, deceiving or missing the expectation that you created.'

Mark Connolly

Ollie Hurry, MD at 2degrees Ltd believes: 'Rapport with different cultures comes from having respect for what's different. I've found that taking time to ask people about their culture and showing real interest in them is far more effective than any courses you can go on or any research you can do. People in this day and age are too concerned with getting something wrong or being disrespectful, rather than actually asking the person directly to share their culture with them.'

Ollie Hurry

Alongside an attitude of openness and respect comes the attitude of generosity. Although giving to others may seem counter-intuitive to achieving your own goals, if you are looking to build long-term connections, it's worth bearing in mind that we are far more likely to remember the person who helped us out than the person who was only out for what they could get. Generosity need not be a costly exercise – we tend to be suspicious of an overblown, expensive gesture – and can be as simple as paying a heartfelt compliment, giving a piece of valuable advice, or recommending a book or film you think they will enjoy.

Linked to generosity is a decision to put to one side, for a while, your own agenda, purpose, goals, targets and objectives: a decision to be present. In emptying your mind you will be free to truly understand their needs and wants, as well as the challenges that keep them up at night. These insights are incredibly valuable whether your aim is to build a connection, motivate a team, or get to know a prospective client. It is only once you have seen the world through their eyes that you will be able to connect with them deeply. You will then be able to identify how you might be able to help them and find solutions that will be beneficial to you both.

······················
Exercise
······················

The ability to build rapport is not something that you can just switch on and off; it's an attitude. To enhance your rapport with current and new connections, practise the following techniques:

1   Think about a person or relationship where you'd like to develop rapport. Imagine that you already have a strong connection and picture what that would be like: maybe you are laughing, nodding, debating with one another. By thinking in this way you will adopt a more open attitude when you meet in real life which will invite a similar response in return.

2   Practise having conversations with people where your only intention is to understand the world from their point of view. Notice the impact that your open approach has on their attitude towards you.

3   As well as taking steps to understand the world from the other person's point of view, find ways to share your own experiences, thoughts and feelings in a way that will be entertaining and informative to them. With every connection that you would like

to make think win/win. Consider what their purpose might be and how your individual goals could complement one another.

4 Practise building rapport not only with people you are naturally attracted to (often people who have similar lifestyles, values and beliefs to you) but also people who don't catch your eye, or even people who for some reason put you off. I have been amazed at how enriching I've found connections with people who I may initially have passed by, purely because they were not like me or didn't attract my initial attention.

5 Approach all interactions with an intention of generosity. Whether at the supermarket checkout or chatting in the lift at work, aim to create an enriching experience for you both, that's appropriate to the context. Notice the impact that your generosity has on your ability to build rapport.

Communicating with rapport

In addition to adopting the right mindset your ability to connect will be based on how skilful you are at communicating with others. Effective communication is a balance between listening – really tuning into what the person is saying – and talking: sharing information and views in a way that is appreciated by others.

Effective listening

People who are adept at building rapport are excellent listeners, whether face to face or on a call. Although the temptation when speaking to someone for the first time may be to talk about yourself, rapport is most effectively developed when you focus your attention on the other person.

The impact of listening was eloquently illustrated in an experiment when a coach travelling on the middle seat of an aeroplane was briefed to simply ask passengers sitting on either side questions about themselves. The coach's fellow travellers were then asked, as they came off the flight, what they thought of him. Unanimously, they reported that they found him a fascinating person with an interesting life, even though he had not actually shared any information about himself at all!

Peter Reilly

Peter Reilly, Commercial Director at STV is a charismatic leader and often described as the life and soul of a party. However, he believes rapport is most effectively built when you ask relevant questions and listen attentively to the answers. 'When I meet people for the first time, I'm consciously quieter than I normally would be. I know I can be a bit outspoken at times and aware that people may not get my sense of humour or the tone I'm pitching it at. If you want to build solid relationships and you want people to remember you, get them to talk about themselves.'

Being listened to is an enriching experience, particularly because it happens so rarely. We think we listen, but most of the time we interject, interpret, interrupt or ignore. With the best will in the world we don't give the person time to finish off their sentences and instead jump in with advice, recommendations, or our own experiences.

Truly listening pays dividends when you've just started a role, as a way of navigating the lay of the land. It's invaluable during times of change: to help people feel appreciated and give them the opportunity to share concerns. It's crucial during one-to-ones and group meetings to ensure you draw views from everyone and give them the attention they deserve. It's an invaluable life skill that will make you remembered, respected and liked by people at any level. When a person is fully tuned into what you're saying, acknowledging what you've said with no judgement or commentary, you feel valued and respected. When people feel listened to, they relax and share more of their authentic self.

If you are looking to hone your listening skills the first step is to 'switch on'. Remind yourself of the overall purpose for being there and if the conversation is worth having, allow yourself enough time to give it your full attention and get your mind, body and spirit 'in the room'. You should then allow your curiosity to flourish by asking open questions that foster exploration (e.g. why, what, how and what if?) rather than closed questions that invite an immediate conclusion.

Once you have asked your question, the next step is to listen carefully to the response. Use active listening to demonstrate that you've heard them, not by repeating every single word, but by reflecting the essence of what they've said, using key words they've chosen. Use probing questions to seek clarification and show that you really want to understand their views and respond with a mixture of words, noises and gestures to encourage them to open up. Noises like 'uh hu', 'mmm' or words like 'ok', 'yes' and 'and' are effective, as are nodding, smiling, putting your head on one side and subtly raising your eyebrows. Take your time to observe not only what the person is saying, but how they are saying it. Listen not only with your ears, but with your eyes and body. Does their body language support their words, or are their eyes, facial expression or posture telling a different story? What do the tone of their voice, the speed at which they are talking, their pauses and inflections say about their inner thoughts and feelings?

The best questions often take the most time to answer. You will know when you've asked a powerful questions as you'll often get a response like 'that's a good question...' or they may look away and go quiet. Rather than jumping in to fill the silence, give them time to answer and enjoy the 'ahaaa' effect when they have a light bulb moment.

For a deep level of rapport to occur, the key is to put aside for a while your own perspective and put yourself in the other person's shoes. Key to objective listening is to avoid jumping to conclusions, adding in your own perspective or finishing off people's sentences. Instead, aim to see the world through their eyes. As you do so, you may naturally start to communicate in the same way as they do – mirroring their posture, breathing patterns, choice of words, pace and volume. This should occur naturally as a result of your increasing rapport. Beware of mirroring as a ploy to instigate rapport too early as people will sense that you're not being genuine.

Once the conversation is over, reflect on the little details that you found interesting and unique. Knowing that you've been heard by someone is a real gift. Your ability to remember gems from previous conversations will demonstrate that you were genuinely interested in them as a person and that you valued their point of view.

Effective talking

As well as being excellent listeners, people who build rapport are adept at the art of 'making' conversation. This skill may appear to be entirely spontaneous; however the best conversationalists have often thought about who they will be meeting, prepared suitable topics of conversation in advance and honed their stories to perfection.

Effective conversations are all about creating touch points – the bright sparks that trigger and enliven a fulfilling conversation. You can think about these touch points as though they were layers in an iceberg, with the surface layer representing the most accessible and safest touch points and the deeper layers representing the thoughts and feelings hidden beneath the surface.

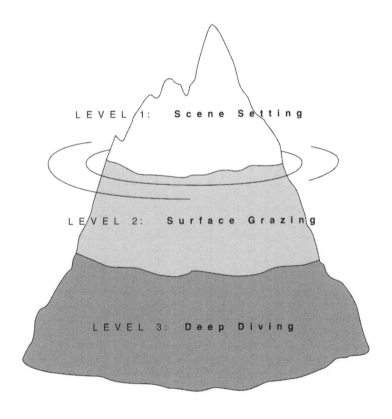

LEVEL 1:   Scene Setting

LEVEL 2:   Surface Grazing

LEVEL 3:   Deep Diving

Because every person is different, it is important to adopt an open and flexible approach to conversation, respect the level at which they would like to converse and have a broad range of topics to share. The diagram below provides an overview of the range of conversation touch points that you can access to ignite a conversation at three levels, which I've called 'scene setting', 'surface grazing' and 'deep diving'.

Level 1: Scene setting. At this point, you're just opening up the conversation. Although these are light topics, they are a great way of breaking the ice. Conversations sometimes need time to warm up and so jumping this level could come across as quite direct and possibly even frighten people off. Topics could include the weather, their journey, general 'how are yous?' and genuine compliments.

Bridging: Unless the whole purpose of your conversation is to create surface level rapport, there will come a point in the conversation when one of you will want to move it to the next stage. An effective way of doing this is by introducing a bridging phrase, which illustrates your overall purpose, highlights any common ground that you share and steers the conversation in that direction.

Level 2: Surface grazing. This level follows on from the scene setting and provides substance for the conversation. When you meet someone for the first time, you may undergo a mutual 'fishing expedition' where you explore touch points and uncover common areas of interests. Topics may include business – latest developments at work, global/national business news, either person's subject matter expertise; people – figures in the public eye or mutual acquaintances, taking care to avoid gossip as this is one of the quickest ways to lose gravitas; history – respective backgrounds, shared experiences, historical facts of note for the day; geography – your current location, where they're from, holidays; current affairs – the day's news, topics relevant to both parties or humour – storytelling or jokes, although delivered sparingly and with respect.

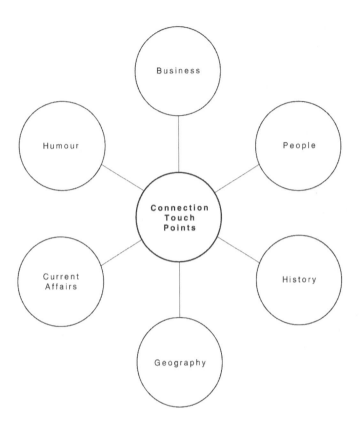

Level 3: Deep diving. Moving to a deeper level of conversation should be initiated with care. Whereas one person will be ready to have a profound conversation the first time you meet, another will be less inclined to veer from the surface level. The courage to reveal yourself at a deeper level may alienate some, however it may be the factor that differentiates you from the crowd and contributes most to your gravitas. If you feel uncomfortable connecting at a deeper level, particularly in the workplace, you may like to take your lead from the other person. Areas that you could explore include your respective purpose, identity, values and beliefs as they relate to the topic under discussion, your unique point of view, your challenges and how you've overcome them.

Although when people meet for the first time the most obvious approach may be to focus on the positives, the courage to 'share your pain' can be an effective way of demonstrating your authenticity and building trust. Compare the rapport developed following a conversation about the company social or a successful project with the bonds forged over an exchange about the broken down air conditioning or a holiday from hell. This is not an approach that will work with everyone, as some find any admission of difficulty as a sign of weakness and of course it's important for any disclosure to be appropriate to the situation and relationship.

Non-verbal touch points

In addition to the conversational touch points you can use to enrich a conversation, you can also pay attention to the non-verbal signals that build rapport including eye contact, smiling and hand gestures. These are the subtle signs that show you are listening and that you care enough to have a meaningful discussion.

Eyes are known as the 'windows of the soul' and you should aim to make full eye contact for a few seconds at least once during a conversation, and maybe more, depending on how comfortable you both seem with it. A smile is also a disarming gesture that opens people up and can break down even the strongest barriers. Smiles should be genuine and reach beyond your mouth and up to your eyes.

There is a vast array of hand gestures that can create a subtle bond before any words have been exchanged. Reaching out in their direction, placing your hand on the table pointing towards them, touching your own heart to emphasize a point (a "heartfelt gesture") are all techniques to explore. Appropriate touching, of a person's arm or hand, can also make a huge difference to the level of rapport that's created between people. This was demonstrated in an informal study that was conducted in an American diner where the waitress was briefed to touch one group of customers on the arm as she led them to their table and not touch the other group, and compare the tips she received from both groups. The researchers found that the tips were significantly higher in the arm-touching group, indicating that even in neutral situations, physical touch can make a big difference.

Although there are countless ways you can create connections with people, both professionally and personally, I have coached many leaders who feel they have lost that personal touch with their teams, colleagues and families because of the demands of time and high pressure roles. The good news is that with a positive intention, and relatively little time, it is easy to create and rekindle connections, and enjoy the benefits that this brings.

The ability to connect may not be the most obvious route to gravitas and yet, it is integral. When it comes to building gravitas, who you are and how much you share communicates far more eloquently than what you choose to say or do at that moment in time. And whilst it is crucial for leaders to put time and effort into building connections, building rapport and creating meaningful conversations, at the end of the day what matters most is that, when you are face to face with the other person, you let the real you be seen. A person with gravitas is always the same, whether they are talking to their grandchild, the ticket inspector or the chief of the board. Although they may use a different 'language' or tone, they do not let this flexibility compromise who they are and what they stand for.

In choosing to reach out and connect with a broad spectrum of people, you will begin to explore different facets of yourself that you may not have recognised before. In opening yourself up to diverse connections, you will find ways to achieve your purpose, broadening your horizons and opportunities in the process.

Chapter 6

Projection

*'Think good thoughts and they will
shine out of your face like sunbeams
and you will always look lovely.'*

• The Twits, Roald Dahl •

Have you noticed there are some people who command attention
just by being in the room? People who hold an audience spellbound
whenever they deliver a presentation? Who confidently express their
point of view and seem effortlessly to bring others round to their

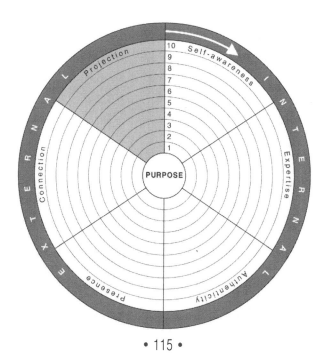

way of thinking? The likelihood is that they have learnt the secrets of projection, which is the final segment of the Gravitas Wheel©.

As a leader with gravitas, there will be times when you have to actively draw attention to yourself to increase your personal impact. Whether in meetings, speaking in public or galvanising a group behind an idea or message, there will be occasions when you will need to assert your opinion, take centre stage and own the room.

The ability to project is the quickest and most direct route to self-expression. Leaders who have mastered the skill radiate an air of confidence, through the way they look, talk and act. In a goldfish bowl world, those who project stand out from the crowd and are remembered long after they have left the building.

Just like the other components of the Gravitas Wheel©, the ability to project can be learnt. Once you have mastered the art of projection, you will find it easier to:
- Communicate with power and impact in meetings
- Command attention in telephone and video conference calls
- Confidently address large audiences

In this chapter, we explore the techniques that enhance projection and how you can use them to maximise your gravitas as a leader.

What is projection?

The term 'projection' is defined as the presentation of an image on a surface, or the ability to make a sound heard at a distance. In both instances there is a piece of information to convey, a sound or image; a medium through which to convey that information and a receiver of that information, an audience.

When it comes to leading with gravitas, projection is the ability to 'switch on' and amplify your message, so that even the largest audiences not only notice you, but give you their undivided attention.

The concept of 'switching on' is beautifully illustrated in a story about Marilyn Monroe, who was out shopping one day with Norman Mailer. Norman expressed surprise that Marilyn wasn't getting her usual attention and she replied that at that moment, she was not 'being Marilyn'. To demonstrate the difference, she flicked a metaphorical switch and 'became' Marilyn, at which point she was instantly mobbed.

The ability to 'flick that switch' is harnessed by actors, performers and public speakers to command attention, rally a crowd and perform at their best. Once the switch is 'on', it occurs in a variety of ways, as illustrated in the table below which compares lack of projection with projection through words, pitch, volume, movement and image.

Words	Compare 'Can everyone listen to me please?' with the gravitas of 'Friends, nobles, countrymen, lend me your ears' (*Julius Caesar*, Shakespeare).
Pitch	Contrast the truncated, disembodied, monotonous voice on the other end of a conference call with the voice of my favourite teacher, whose 'hello' had the rise and fall of a rollercoaster finishing with at least three 'o's and who delighted in enunciating every syllable of 'Feb-ru-ary' so you couldn't help but learn how to spell it!
Volume	Contrast the standard volume of corporate meeting rooms with the voice of an actor, whose range enthrals even the back row of a theatre, whether enacting a loud, heated argument or a soft, gentle soliloquy.
Movement	Compare your colleague's relaxed stroll from desk to printer with the strut and swagger of Freddie Mercury, the energy of Michael Jackson, or the animation of comedians like Michael Macintyre or Billy Connolly.
Image	Contrast the corporate greys, beiges, blacks and navies with the multi-coloured hues of Kids Company's Camila Batmanghelidjh and, at the extreme, the naked image of Gail Porter projected onto the Houses of Parliament in 1999 as a PR stunt for *FHM* magazine.

Although these examples of projection may seem somewhat extreme – no, I'm not asking you to go naked in the office! – they hold the clues to projection in a corporate environment, where the quickest and most direct way to be noticed is to enhance your impact and amplify your delivery. Imagine if you were to bring an element of Shakespeare's gravitas or a fraction of an actor's diction into modern day business speech. Or if you brought a dash of a pop band's vitality or a sprinkle of a diva's sparkle into your communication style. How would you come across and what would be the impact?

As you think about the attention you would like to command as a leader it can be helpful to think about projection as an amplified and augmented version of presence. As discussed in Chapter 4, presence is a flame which attracts attention through the intensity of its glow. By contrast, projection is a shining beacon of light which beams energy out across a distance to everyone in the room. With presence, you attract attention purely by being in the room; with projection, you command attention through the power of your delivery. Depending on your message and the number of people you'd like to reach, you can either dial up presence, or turn the gas up until you reach projection.

Once you've decided to project, it is important to consider how much by. Project too much and you may come across as self-centred, ego-driven, or over-bearing. Project too little and you may be perceived as boring, unassertive, or even go completely unnoticed. To help you decide what's appropriate you can think about projection as levels on a dial, as illustrated below.

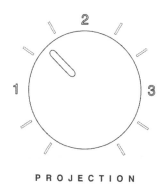

PROJECTION

Level 1 Projection includes making a memorable impression in a meeting or commanding attention during a telephone or video conference.

Level 2 Projection includes delivering a presentation to a small to medium sized group or making an announcement to your team.

Level 3 Projection includes delivering a speech to a large audience, either in an auditorium or via satellite link up.

Amplifying your delivery

The first step in learning how to project is to become aware of those situations when ramping up your delivery would be beneficial. For building gravitas, this might include giving a speech to a large audience, asserting yourself with a challenging client, presenting your most confident self during a job interview or making a powerful impact with the chairman of the board. Although the temptation in these situations may be to 'wing it' without any preparation at all, this can result in a sense of disappointment where you end up thinking 'I could have done so much better...', 'I really let myself down then...', 'They didn't see the real me...'

People who project best are those actors and performers who only appear in front of their audience once they have learnt a script, taken professional direction and rehearsed until word perfect. If you are looking to have an equivalent level of impact in front of your audiences, why would you risk winging it?

Exercise

To ensure you are as prepared as possible, begin by identifying those situations when you would like to project, the audiences you will be coming into contact with, what they will be expecting from you and how you would like to come across to them. As well as considering the people, think about the environment you're in and tailor your level of projection accordingly. For example, if you're presenting to a thousand delegates you will need to project more than if you are chairing a meeting of ten people.

Situation where projection is required	Audience profile, attitude and expectations	Environment /location	How I would like to come across	Level of projection required (1, 2 or 3)
Example 1: Delivering a presentation to the board	5-7 board members; some sceptical about the message I'm about to deliver	Meeting room; participants sat around a boardroom table; presenters usually stood or seated at the front	In control, confident, calm, subject matter expertise. Potential scepticism overcome through reasoned logic	Level 1
Example 2: Delivering a 10 minute keynote speech at a congress	Audience of 200+ informed delegates; attitude towards your message unknown	Congress venue; speech to be delivered from a lectern using a lapel mike	Informed, serious yet relaxed, authentic; expertise illustrated through credentials and anecdotes	Level 3

Create a table like the one above to profile the various situations when you would like to project, your audiences and their expectations, the environment or location and how you would like to come across. In the final column, you can then record the level of projection that will be required, from 1 to 3.[21] You can use the examples to prompt your thinking.

Now that you have identified those situations when you would like to project and at which level, we will explore the techniques you can employ to switch on and amplify your impact. We will begin by looking at the energy that drives projection – the power of your mind – and then explore how you can increase projection by using the power of your body and your voice at each of the three levels.

Managing your mindset

Although we may take it for granted, the mind is a powerful tool that we can manage to achieve the results we want. Think for a moment how easy it is to trigger an emotion of sadness just by watching a sad film or remembering an unhappy event. In the same way, you can choose to create a positive state of mind simply by shifting your focus to times when you have felt confident and strong.

When it comes to projecting gravitas, people's perception of you is directly influenced by how you see yourself. When you see yourself as a leader with gravitas whose purpose and message deserve attention that is exactly how you will come across.

As well as harnessing positive thoughts, be aware of your internal dialogue and its impact on your confidence. What happens to your emotional state when you tell yourself that you're stupid or inarticulate or, by contrast, smart and engaging? How does your perception of a future audience change when you replace the word 'hostile' with the word 'engaged'? Consider too the words you use when describing yourself to others. Are you modest, self-

---

[21] For an online version of this table, go to www.leadingwithgravitas.com/resources.

deprecating or do you veer on the downright negative? When recounting past experiences, do you focus on what went well, or the mistakes you made? Learning how to manage your mindset will ensure that you remain focused and keep negative influences at bay, whether you're preparing for a specific event or thinking about life in general.

Mary was a recently appointed manager of a large retail outlet. She came to me for coaching as she was concerned about how she could make her mark at a potentially hostile shareholders' meeting. In preparing for the meeting, Mary's immediate plan was to devote additional time to enhancing her slides. Although we agreed she needed to build a strategy to fend off shareholders' concerns, we decided that just as important was getting her into the most positive mindset to project her best self.

As Mary thought about the meeting she realised that she was allowing her mind to focus on all those times when she felt she believed she'd made 'stupid' comments, or when she'd been shouted down. As she thought about the upcoming meeting, she pictured herself surrounded by an aggressive group, desperately trying to defend herself. Instead of thinking these disempowering thoughts, Mary decided to shift her attention to meetings when she had confidently delivered her message, the recent projects that had delivered outstanding results, and the times when she had successfully navigated challenging meetings. She consequently went into the meeting prepared to project her most confident self – and received a welcoming response from the shareholders who appreciated her upbeat style.

Mary

As well as visualising and replaying positive highlights, you can ask yourself 'success-seeking' questions to make the most of situations when you have projected with gravitas. Compare the effect that questions like 'What did I do well?' or 'What can I learn from this?' have on your confidence, with questions like 'What did I do wrong?' or 'Why does this always happen to me?' This approach will maintain focus on how far you have come and help you to identify what you can do to progress even further in the future. As you identify and reinforce memories of when you have been at your best, you will create a virtual library of positive events that you can access whenever preparing for upcoming events.

Another effective technique for expanding your comfort zone is to 'act' as if you were already projecting at the level you would like. If you want to have the gravitas of Laurence Olivier, the magnetism of Elvis Presley or the presence of Greta Garbo, consider how they think, speak, stand and dress – and then step into that role. In choosing to adopt characteristics of people you admire you will broaden your range of expression and enhance your own authentic communication style.

Another technique to project your best self and stop nerves from getting the better of you is creating a set of 'anchors' that you can use to access your most powerful inner resources. A classic example of anchoring is the bow-and-arrow pose that Usain Bolt strikes before the start of a race. More subtle examples are the rituals that actors, musicians and public speakers perform before going on stage, for example reciting a set of words or making a specific gesture to trigger a desired emotion.

Creating your own anchors, and knowing how to trigger them, can be a great way to generate the most resourceful state for whatever situation you are about to face. You can create a whole range of anchors for different situations. For example, if you'd like to deliver a serious message, you may like to trigger a sombre mindset. Alternatively, you may like to deliver an entertaining presentation and so would choose a light-hearted, humorous state of mind. Using these anchors can help you stay relaxed, confident, positive, energised, calm – whatever emotional state you want – despite what might be going on around you.[22]

Projecting through your body and voice

As well as getting yourself into the most conducive mindset to project with gravitas, increasing awareness of the messages you're sending out through your body and voice and adapting them to suit different situations will have a massive impact on how your gravitas is perceived.

In the same way as birds puff up their chests, cats arch their backs and dogs raise their hackles to ward off predators, you can adopt techniques to make yourself bigger and louder to command attention and handle potentially challenging situations. With open body language you can send out subliminal messages of confidence and ease; with closed body language you can shut people off, appearing at one extreme timid and at the other arrogant or even aggressive.

Likewise, the way you use your breath and voice will hugely affect your impact. Our bodies are designed to make noise, with sound resonating from our lungs, vocal chords, chest, mouth, tongue, teeth and lips. For maximum projection we need to override the messages to "shush" and "be quiet" that we've received since birth and enjoy the range and breadth of our vocal chords.

We will now explore the techniques you can access to project at levels 1, 2 and 3.

---

[22] For more guidance on anchors, read *NLP at Work*, Sue Knight, Nicholas Brealey Publishing.

Level 1 Projection

Situations requiring Level 1 Projection include making a strong and powerful impression during a meeting and commanding attention in a telephone or video conference call.

A great tip used by telephone sales people is to stand up, as this immediately builds psychological strength and enhances your ability to project. If standing is not appropriate, think about where to position yourself in the room for maximum impact. If you have a choice, arrive early and sit at the head of the table, giving you a superior position and a strong vantage point from which to see and be seen. Alternatively, choose a seat facing the door, so that you are the first to greet everyone as they walk in.

The way you sit will either enhance or detract from your ability to project gravitas. Sit right back in the chair, with both feet on the ground. Having a symmetrical posture will demonstrate strength and solidity; crossing your legs or slouching will give the impression of imbalance or sloppiness.

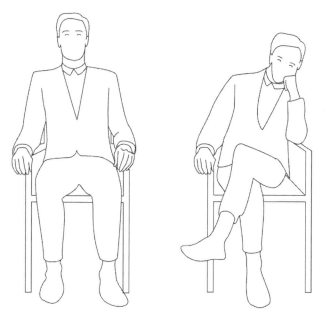

At the beginning of the meeting, make eye contact with everyone in the room: not fleetingly, like most people do, but for a couple of seconds and whilst doing so, think about the interesting conversations that you will have with each of them.

When you want to actively participate in the conversation, lean forward into the group space, placing your arms on the table, in an open rather than crossed position. If you are struggling to make yourself heard, use the hand you write with to 'cut into' the conversation. This is effectively using your hand as a silencer, without the negative connotations of pointing or using your hand as a stop sign. Accompany your hand gesture with 'building phrases' such as 'that's a great point, David, and I'd like to add to it by saying…' Using the person's name acknowledges them personally and can take away the sting of being interrupted. Using "and" rather than "but" (even though you may not entirely agree with what's come before) is another useful technique for maintaining rapport while bringing your own perspective into the conversation.

As well as using your body, your ability to project will be greatly enhanced when you engage the power of your voice. This is not about shouting, which in fact the most impactful communicators avoid. It's about working with the full range of your voice. Filling your lungs with air before you speak will give you the 'fuel' to put your point across and the capacity to increase your volume. To keep the attention on you, make sure you maintain volume to the end of your sentences, rather than fading off.

Consider too the pace of your voice. Speak slowly and you'll sound confident in your message. Speak fast and you'll either appear nervous or sound like you don't value what you're saying. Take care to enunciate your words: mumbling, mispronouncing or cutting words short gives the impression of laziness, and can result in the meaning getting lost somewhere between your mouth and your chin. Conversely, pronouncing every syllable will make it much easier for you to project outwards, with the added bonus of building self-confidence with every word you speak.

Another effective technique for keeping the audience focused on you is the numbering technique: 'there are three considerations: firstly... secondly... and thirdly...' Not only does this convey clarity of thought, it also prevents interruptions.

Take care not to detract from your message with fillers such as 'sort of', 'you know what I mean' or 'I guess'; disqualifiers like 'I'm not sure if this is right, but...', 'I probably didn't make myself clear then' or 'does that make sense?'; or verbal ticks like 'ummm', 'urrr', 'so' or 'like'. These often creep in when you're nervous, unclear or searching for the next thing to say, but can easily become a habit. They indicate a lack of confidence and can be hugely distracting to your audience. Ask a friend or colleague to video you to identify to what extent you use fillers in your speech. The goal shouldn't necessarily be to eliminate them altogether. In fact, I once worked with an MD who had ironed out every verbal nuance in his delivery to the point where he came across as cold and robotic. The goal should be to ensure that they don't detract from your message.

If you would like to cut down on verbal fillers, a surprisingly quick and effective solution is to prepare your thoughts in advance and decide to replace your verbal ticks with silence. This gives your audience time to process what you've just said and is much easier on the ear.

Projecting in a conference call or video conference

In a global business environment, it's likely that many meetings will be held via conference call. Whilst many people view these as an opportunity to eat their lunch, catch up on emails and work on other projects, they can be a highly effective means of leading from afar. Rather than going with the flow and wasting a large part of your day sitting on calls, decide to make the ones you participate in concise and engaging by using the following tips:

1 Circulate an agenda in advance which clearly states everyone's roles and responsibilities for the call.
2 State up front how much time will be spent on each section of the agenda.
3 Make the calls interactive and invite comments from participants throughout rather than at the end, so that they stay focused all the way through.
4 Inject extra energy into your voice and maintain the pace: speak simply, clearly and with minimal jargon.
5 For video conferences, maintain eye contact, avoid jerky movements and ensure your facial expressions can be easily read and are consistent with your words.

Level 2 Projection

Level 2 Projection is required when delivering a presentation to a small to medium sized group or making an announcement to your team. In these situations, you will want to add to the techniques covered in Level 1 through your breath, voice and body.

Your breath creates the energy that drives you and is directly linked to your ability to project. Effective breathing will ensure your brain has sufficient oxygen to think and communicate clearly.

Controlled breathing is a skill which will increase your vocal range, give you a powerful and strong voice, help to calm nerves and anxiety and ensure you're projecting at your best. Standing or sitting in a relaxed, neutral position, place your hands at the base of your ribs with your middle fingers touching. Take a deep, steady breath in and concentrate on expanding the air into the space below your hands. Rather than breathing 'vertically', where your shoulders will move upwards and air will come into the top of your lungs, concentrate on breathing 'horizontally', where your rib cage expands outwards as you draw air deeper into the bottom of your lungs. As you do this, you should see your middle fingers moving away from one another as your lungs expand. Notice the impact that the deeper breathing has on your voice, your ability to project and your state of mind.

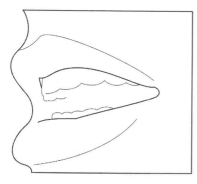

Having mastered the art of controlled breathing, you will have more control over your voice, so that you can select the most appropriate pitch, volume and pace to suit the situations. When describing a person with gravitas, one of the key characteristics often cited is their voice. A voice without gravitas is often thin and reedy, either high pitched or flat and monotone. By contrast, a voice with gravitas is deep and resonant; its tone is measured and rich, with words spoken clearly and without haste.

Clarity of speech conveys clarity of thought and so for maximum impact, plan what you're going to say in advance and practice out loud until you feel confident.

As you practice your level 2 delivery, think about where you can speed up, for example telling funny stories or reviewing background information, and where you can slow down, perhaps to emphasise key words or points of note. Also bear in mind the power of the pause. Whether deliberately designed into a presentation or incorporated on the spot to give you time to collect your thoughts, a moment of silence is a highly effective way of demonstrating gravitas. People will assume you are a deep thinker and look forward to the moment you choose to speak.

You can also vary your volume of speech to inject different levels of emotion. Speaking loudly will express passion and intensity whereas speaking quietly will draw your audience in. If you would like to command attention on a call or at a meeting, begin by speaking more loudly than others. You can then use the teacher's trick of decreasing your volume, which will encourage your audience to lean in and focus more carefully on what you're saying.

For added vocal colour, incorporate inflection into your delivery, using the highs and lows of your voice to illustrate the ups and downs of your message. For gravitas, beware the *Neighbours* factor, which turns every statement into a question and can give the impression that you're not sure of anything.

Before going into situations which require you to project, take the time to warm up your voice, making sure you're somewhere private first!

1 Take a few 'horizontal' breaths, drawing air down into your lungs and towards your diaphragm.

2 Warm up your mouth and tongue with the classic actors' trick of chewing an imaginary stick of gum which gets bigger and smaller the more you chew it.

3 Focus on projecting sound out from your chest, across the 'mask' of your face as well as through your throat and mouth. Try saying 'mmmmm' while feeling the sound emanating from every part of you.

4 Pick a favourite nursery rhyme, poem or phrase and recite it, out loud, over-enunciating every syllable.

5 To project commandingly, use the consonants to help you break up your words. Relish the sound and inject power and personality into every syllable.

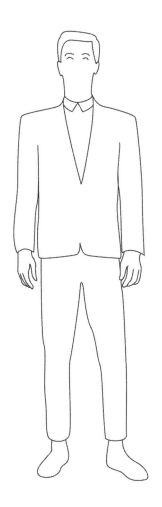

A powerful complement to a voice with gravitas is a body that projects energy. Many business presentations are now delivered seated, with the presenter clicking through slides from their laptop and their audience, having glanced nervously at the slide counter, hypnotised by a monotonous display of numbers and words. If you are looking to project memorably, I encourage you to break this mould. Instead of sitting, stand up, at the front of the room. If you need to share slides, keep them short and sweet and send out a detailed version later if required.

The way you hold your body as you stand will have a tremendous impact on your confidence. Rather than slouching on one hip, as many women do, or crossing your feet, which makes you look unsteady and

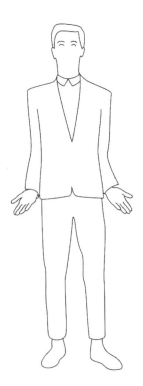

unsure, plant your feet directly under your hips. This will keep you balanced and grounded, and convey strength and solidity. Then imagine that there is a string pulling you up from the top of your head. This will give you a straight and symmetrical posture and encourage your shoulders to relax down and back.

Arms and hand movements will also greatly enhance your projection, especially when communicating with larger audiences. For formal presentations, begin by holding your arms in a neutral position, as opposed to by your sides or behind your back, which can look too regimented or guarded. You can then gesture outwards to emphasize your points. Remember that the bigger the gesture, the greater the emphasis. Gesturing with your palms down will express seriousness and trustworthiness; gesturing palms up gives a more light-hearted impression and should be used sparingly as it can convey weakness and diminish your status.

You can also use your hands to emphasize your words, for example, if you're talking about 'a massive increase in sales' highlight the 'massiveness' with your arms outstretched. If you're talking about an increase in sales from 10 percent to 90 percent indicate the difference by increasing the gap between your hands.

Level 3 Projection

Projecting at level 3 is required when you are delivering a speech to a large audience, either from a lectern, podium or via satellite. While all the points covered in levels 1 and 2 are relevant here, there are a number of techniques you can employ to amplify your message even further so that you can engage with the biggest crowds.

Although it may feel like you're addressing a sea of blank faces, eye contact is crucial. Avoid fixing your attention on one spot, which looks like favouritism and minimises your connection to the rest of the room. Also, avoid 'lighthouse sweeping' your gaze from side to side which can be unnerving for your audience. Instead, divide the room up into sections and imagine that you are talking to a supportive colleague or friend located in each section. Even though you may not be able to read their facial expressions from a distance, look them in the eye, hold their gaze for the time it takes for your point to land, and then move onto the next person.

Paying particular attention to your vocal delivery will ensure that even the largest groups stay engaged. As with all levels of projection, breathe deeply and calmly into your diaphragm to ensure you bring out the full resonance of your voice. As part of your rehearsal, go out onto the stage and practice 'throwing' your voice, like a ball, to different locations in the room. This will encourage you to speak to your whole audience and convey confidence and strength.

When addressing a larger crowd, it's important to plan ahead how you want your audience to feel and adapt your own energy accordingly. If you want to express passion and strength, build rapid physical movement into your performance; if you want to portray vitality and enthusiasm, put a spring into your step as you move around the stage and incorporate vocal variety into your delivery; for weight and gravitas, slow down your speech, deepen your tone and make your movements precise and deliberate.

To build in variety, consider slightly exaggerating your gestures and facial expressions to emphasise key points. Watch how actors and comedians do it, or take a leaf from the book of footballers who method act their discomfort after receiving a yellow card. Movement is good, but make sure you do it with a purpose, rather than drifting from one place to the next. Create 'spatial anchors' in different places on the stage and associate key points with each of those places. For example, when talking about activities that occurred in the past, stand on the audience's left; for the future, move to their right; you can also use different spots on the stage to talk about different concepts or characters. Keep your posture open: avoid folding your arms, standing behind a lectern or turning your back on the audience.

The words you choose will either enhance or detract from your projection. Make sure you display a genuine interest in the information you are presenting through using phrases like 'I'm delighted to tell you', signposting words like 'the key take-home point here is' and modelling the reaction you'd like your audience to have with phrases such as 'the latest data is fascinating', 'I found this information deeply alarming. I think you will too'.

Use the techniques in the Connection Chapter to maintain rapport while you project. Choose to have a conversation with your audience, however large, by asking open and rhetorical questions. Imagine you know people in the audience, and 'listen' to their reaction through reading their body language and sensing the atmosphere in the room.

Make your presentation memorable and ignite your audience's imagination with the power of your words. Rather than saying 'I'm pleased to tell you we have exceeded our targets by 10 percent', try the following multisensory phrases: 'I know you'll be delighted to *hear* that we've exploded our target by 10 percent. If you *look* at our individual contributions over the past year as illustrated in this beautiful graph, you'll *see* that it's been down to each and every one of you. I *feel* proud of everything you've done for the company. As we look to our future plans, I feel refreshed and invigorated by our combined success'.

Have fun with your presentations, and inject a poet's lyricism, a comedian's wit or a game-show host's catch phrases into your talk, whilst ensuring your message and delivery are appropriately tailored to each audience you meet.

As well as thinking about the individual words, take time to structure your presentation to make it memorable. Begin by identifying the key message you would like your audience to walk away with. Consider: if your presentation were front page news what would be the headline? Your introduction should then map out the presentation for your audience: 'First I'm going to talk to you about X, then we're going to explore Y and then we'll finish off with Z.' You can then take your audience by the hand and lead them through each section, making sure to recap where you're at as you go through, and then summarise the main points at the end.

As part of your talk, you can also acknowledge the size of the room, and the people sitting in it: 'It's great to see so many people here…', 'Can you all hear me at the back?' or 'I can tell from looking at your faces as you came in that today's going to be a great day… '

As you plan your structure, also consider using the rule of three to signpost the way – 'there are three points I'd like to make: point one… point two… and point three… ', then going through each point in turn and finishing up with a recap of all three points. You could also incorporate the classic hero's journey which describes a three-part adventure where the hero firstly has a desire, secondly encounters a roadblock which involves a struggle or choice, and finally emerges transformed. Although this might sound more like a children's story, it is a highly memorable method of sharing a case study. For example: 'Five years ago, we launched an innovative product line, yet struggled to achieve cut through in a competitive marketplace. We struggled for a few years before focusing our attention on just one of our products. Today, that product is market leader and we have tripled our income...'

The words you choose can also draw your audience in: for example: 'I know people have travelled from all over to be here. I'd like to welcome the team from... ' Clever use of questioning and gestures will ensure you interact with all members of the audience, and keep them personally involved in your message: 'How many of you have been affected by the recent changes?' You can also use the game-show host's trick of raising your own hand as you ask a question to encourage audience participation, or 'Let's have a show of hands: who agreed with the decision to... ?'

To inject a sense of classical, statesmanlike gravitas to your talk, draw on rhetorical devices employed by orators throughout the ages. Consider *epizeuxis* – repetition of words such as 'education, education, education' or phrases like 'there will be changes at the corporate level, at the team level, and at the individual level'; *anaphora* – repetition of a word or phrase at the start of successive clauses or sentences, for example Winston Churchill's, 'We shall not flag or fail. We shall go on to the end. We shall fight in France, we shall fight on the seas and oceans... We shall never surrender'. You could also try *epistrophe* – repetition of a word or phrase at the end of successive clauses or sentences, for example Emerson's, 'What lies behind us and what lies before us are tiny compared to what lies within us.'

On the day, avoid reading from slides, notes or cue cards. If you are using a written speech, highlight the key points and words and make sure they are big enough for you to see. If you are using

PowerPoint slides to accompany your presentation, make sure they are visible from every seat in the room. As you present from them, glance briefly at the content and then turn back to your audience. To stop yourself from reading the content, cut down on the words and choose visuals instead.

If you're going to be wearing a microphone, remember that there is no need to increase the volume of your voice. With a hand-held mike, hold it firmly at a distance of approximately 15-20 centimetres from your mouth; with a lapel or lavaliere mike, make sure you wear clothing with a lapel or tie that you can easily clip onto and keep buttons, jewellery and hair out of the way to avoid rustling. If you are incorporating a Q&A session into your presentation, make sure you have sufficient 'roving mikes' available in the audience.

The best way to prepare for any presentation is to rehearse, out loud, in the 'live' venue. Begin by going through the whole talk, ignoring any mistakes or stumbles. Seek feedback from a supportive friend or colleague, and ask them to sit in various locations around the room to check that they can see and hear you. Once you are satisfied, leave a break between rehearsal and delivery and prioritise techniques which will build confidence and bring gravitas into your delivery.

Projecting gravitas through your image

Your ability to project as a leader with gravitas can be greatly enhanced through the image you present to the world. Your appearance sends a message about who you are and, like it or not, people will judge you by what you look like in the first few seconds.

Dressing with gravitas means dressing authentically, not as an imitation of someone else: as Judy Garland said: 'Never be a second-rate version of someone else, be a first-rate version of yourself'. For people to trust you, your image should be a true reflection of who you are. However, if you want to appeal to a diverse group of people, it's important to consider the culture and style of the environment that you're in. Sue Donnelly, international image consultant specialising in authentic styling, recommends the following tips:

1   Dress appropriately: Consider the organisation, industry, dress code and culture, the event you're attending and your role and objectives.

2   Choose quality: Buy the best you can afford. Cheap looking clothes and accessories will never communicate gravitas.

3   Look current: If you look up to date on the outside, you will be seen as up to date on the inside. Successful leaders embrace change and are forward looking.

4   Show impeccable grooming: Gaining respect from others starts with showing respect for yourself. Make sure that anything that isn't covered by clothing is clean and smart.

5   Choose appropriate colours: Colours should flatter your complexion and communicate your intentions. For power and authority, go for a high colour contrast, for example, dark suit, white shirt, red tie; for approachability, go for colours that blend pleasingly to the eye, for example, grey suit, pale blue shirt/blouse.

6   Authenticity is key: Clothes should express your personality and what you want to tell the world about yourself. Dress in styles that suit your body shape and colouring; wear clothes that feel good, look good and give you confidence.

Developing a signature style will help you to build a personal brand that says dependability, reliability and gravitas. In choosing to adopt a certain style, make sure that the messages you express through your clothes are consistent with how you want to be seen as a leader.

Now that we have explored the range of techniques you can use to project yourself, it's worth bearing in mind the one thing that may enhance your gravitas more than anything else, which is knowing when not to say anything at all.

In a noisy and frenetic world, when everyone is clamouring to be noticed and heard, sometimes the best approach is to remain still and calm, let your silence speak volumes and know that it may sometimes be the clearest indication of gravitas there is.

Chapter 7

Modelling Leaders with Gravitas

*'We do not act rightly because we have
virtue or excellence, but we rather have
those because we have acted rightly. We
are what we repeatedly do. Excellence,
then, is not an act but a habit.'*

• Aristotle •

Modelling is a useful tool to help you define and hone your own
leadership style and gravitas. It can help you to replicate behaviour
that you admire in others and 'what works' in your own approach.

Modelling can also help you to turn what could be perceived as
'lucky' or 'gifted' behaviour into a series of capabilities and skills you
can learn and then reproduce at will. In this way, when you
experience a time when you felt, or were told, that you demonstrated
gravitas and leadership, you can look back and ask, what was I
doing, thinking and feeling that gave that impression? Likewise,
when you observe a leader who embodies gravitas, you can examine
how they are making such an impact and which qualities you can
adopt to enhance your own style.

Begin by identifying someone you would like to model who you
feel exemplifies leadership and gravitas. Ideally, they will be in the
public eye and a 'real person' as opposed to a character played by an
actor. Alternatively, you could identify a selection of people who
exemplify segments on the Gravitas Wheel©.

Conduct some background research on your gravitas 'exemplar'. Find a selection of clips of them on the internet. Begin by considering which qualities they exemplify on the Gravitas Wheel© and in what way:

- Expertise
- Self-awareness
- Authenticity
- Presence
- Connection
- Projection

As you think about how they come across, consider their leadership identity, as it shows up in their environment, behaviours, skills and capabilities and especially in their values and beliefs, identity and purpose. An excellent tool for this is the Logical Levels of Change model in the *Self-awareness* chapter. You can also model how they come across through what you see, hear and feel. Use the guiding questions below to help you.

What you see
- What do you observe about their body language: posture, facial expressions, arm and hand gestures, position of feet?
- What do you notice about their range of movement: energy, pace, fluidity, symmetry?
- What do you notice about their physical appearance: face, body shape, clothing?
- What else strikes you about what you see?

What you hear
- What do you notice about their voice: its depth, resonance, pace?
- What strikes you about their choice of words, the way they punctuate their speech, the rise and fall of their voice, its melodic quality?

- What impact does their accent have on you and your perception of them?
- What do you notice about what they choose to say, and when they choose to remain silent?
- What do you notice about the way they breathe? Is their breathing deep or shallow? Slow or rapid? Regular or erratic? Conscious or unconscious?
- What else is it about what you hear that contributes to their gravitas?

What you feel

- What physical reactions – if any – do you have in their presence?
- If you were to translate their gravitas into a temperature, what would that be?
- What emotions do you experience when you are in their presence?
- What is that person doing – consciously or unconsciously – to trigger that response in you?
- What else do you feel when you witness their leadership and gravitas?

Now identify those characteristics you would like to develop in yourself. Consider how you could 'take on' their gravitas and in which circumstances. Once you have considered what constitutes gravitas for other people, you can turn your attention to modelling your own, unique approach.

Final thoughts

Congratulations on reaching the end of this book. Having read the chapters and worked your way through the exercises, you will now have a far greater insight into your approach to leading with gravitas.

As you move through your career and life, there will be times when certain segments of the Gravitas Wheel© will feel more relevant and important than others. You may find yourself going back to each of the chapters, revisiting the tips and applying the techniques to new challenges and opportunities.

As you go into different situations, you may also want to particularly call on one segment of the Wheel rather than another: for example, *Projection* for large stage presentations; *Self-awareness* and *Expertise* for career changes; *Connection* for reaching out to others; *Authenticity* and *Presence* for those times when you question yourself as a leader and want to reconnect with your best self.

Having come this far, you will have become more and more aware of the one key message that I'd like to leave you with. As a leader, what's important is defining and pursuing what sits at the heart of the Gravitas Wheel© – your purpose. The more you understand and come back to this, the more confident you will become. As your confidence turns into conviction, the more influence and impact you will have and the more people will want to be led by you.

Good luck, and as my best friend always says to me as I prepare to take the next step in life: 'Be fabulous'.

'We must not cease from exploration.
And the end of all our exploring will be
to arrive where we began and to know
the place for the first time.'
• T.S. Eliot •

Acknowledgements

There are a number of people I would like to thank, without whose inspiration and encouragement this book would not be what it is today.

To Sarah Matthew, one of the most eloquent and sparky leaders I know. The first person I spoke to about the concept; a friend who's encouraged me since I penned the first word.

To my teachers: Sue Knight, provocative coach with heart, who stopped me in my tracks and challenged me to evolve; Philip Brew and Colin Brett, who showed me how to be present and just listen; and Kim Hare, who inspired and influenced my facilitation style.

To Kate James, whose presence inspires me whenever she's at the front of the room and Justin Collinge, fire-starter and master of influencing with integrity.

To all the people who supported me in the publication of this book: Julia McCutcheon, who helped me find my writer's voice; to Lucy McCarraher and Christopher Page from Rethink Press, who have made the publishing process relatively simple and to all the leaders who shared their thoughts on leadership and gravitas.

To all the participants on my programmes, in particular those who have put their heart and soul into the learning and those who have been brave enough to share constructive feedback – the root of all my growth and development.

To my parents and brother, Luke, for encouraging me to always do my best.

And last, but by no means least, to Steve, for believing in me and being by my side every step of the way.

The Author

Antoinette Dale Henderson is a leadership communications coach, trainer and author. She regularly speaks on leadership identity, authenticity in the workplace, building inner confidence and promoting the cause of women in leadership.

Her personal mission is enabling leaders from all walks of life to fulfil their true potential, both in work and outside. In 2007, she launched Zomi Communications to commit to that mission, working with people to identify their purpose and define their unique leadership voice. Her style is described as direct, inspiring, challenging, positive and empowering.

She now works globally with organisations to deliver energising programmes that deliver measurable business results. Particular areas of expertise include leadership development, communication excellence and impact and influencing skills, delivered via group workshops and one-to-one coaching.

Before founding her company, Antoinette spent 18 years holding senior positions at many of the world's top PR agencies, including Ogilvy & Mather, Hill & Knowlton and Weber Shandwick. She is an accredited coach with the International Coaching Federation and Master Practitioner in Neuro Linguistic Programming.

She lives in South-East London with her husband, Steve, and her two daughters, Zoë and Mia. In her spare time, she loves country walks, foreign travel, music, art and sharing delicious food with family and friends.

Further information on the Leading with Gravitas programme, the Gravitas Profiling Questionnaire© and other useful resources can be found on the Leading with Gravitas